A Step by Step Guide to

BOOK PRODUCTION

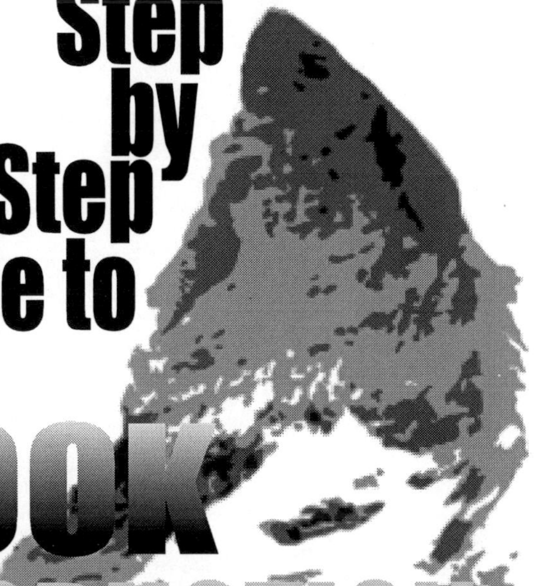

Compiled by
MORRIS LUNDIN

MORI STUDIO SOUTHWEST
Fountain Hills, Arizona

About the cover: The Matterhorn, rising high above Zermatt, Switzerland, represents a challenge for the adventuresome and a pinnacle attainable by methodical, hard work. One goal in book publishing is to reach a peak of sales success. Another goal for the author/publisher is to hold a bound book in one's hand with the exhilaration and self-satisfaction of a project completed "just because it is there!"   —*Photo by Morris Lundin*

Production specifications for this book:
Cover and Text Design: Mori Studio Southwest
Illustrations: Mori Studio Southwest
Text type: Times and Helvetica Regular
Headings: Goudy Bold and Helvetica Bold
Page Layout: PageMaker
Line Art: Adobe Illustrator
Cover: Adobe Photoshop, Adobe Illustrator
Printing: Digital printing by Sir Speedy Scottsdale

A Step-by-Step Guide to Book Production,
     copyright © 2004 by Morris Lundin
First edition, titled *Book Production Encapsulated,*
     copyright © 2003 by Morris Lundin
All rights reserved. Printed in the United States of America.

ISBN 0-9679349-4--X

Library of Congress Control Number: 2004111211

Contact:
Morris Lundin, Mori Studio Southwest,
12828 N. Mountainside Dr., #102, Fountain Hills, AZ 85268
Phone: 480-816-4407; e-mail: morrislundin4407@msn.com

Contents

Parts of a Book

Preliminary pages

- *Half title* — optional; the first page of a book, more often in case bound books, contains only the title and subtitle.
- *Title page* — contains title, subtitle, authors name and affiliation, publisher's logo.
- *Copyright page* — contains copyright notice, ISBN, Library of Congress Control Number or Cataloguing-in-Publication data as applicable, country where printed, sometimes the publisher's address and contact info. May also list the publisher's editorial and production staff.
- *Dedication* — optional; dedication of the book to a person or persons who inspired the author.
- *Table of Contents* — a listing of chapters which should match the exact wording of the chapter headings and the pages on which they begin. In textbooks, subdivisions in each chapter could also be listed.
- *List of illustrations or tables* — optional; may also list credits and permissions for borrowed material.
- *Foreword* — note correct spelling; may be written by a person other than the author.
- *Preface* — author's description of the book's purpose.
- *Acknowledgments* — gives credit to persons who may have helped author with the book; may be part of the preface.

Text

- *Parts* — main topics into which several chapters can be grouped.
- *Chapters* — main topics.
- *Headings and subheadings* — bold or large type indicating a hierarchy of subdivisions of text.
- *Running heads* — usually book title on even numbered (verso) pages, chapter title on odd numbered (recto) pages; placed above the text at the top of each page except chapter openers.
- *Folios* — page numbers, usually placed top right and left or bottom centered; odd numbers on right pages, even numbers on left.

Back Matter

- *Appendix* — items that support text but do not warrant an entire chapter.
- *Glossary* — definitions of important terms
- *Bibliography* — a list of resources from which the author extracted information.
- *Index* — a list of terms with page number where found.

Preface

The printed word is still the prevalent means of preserving and disseminating ideas at the beginning of the Twenty-First Century. The body of information contained in a book is analogous to the human body. The basic idea is the *skeleton*—the framework on which the rest of the organism is built The outward appearance of the book is like the *skin*—it is the attribute that is visible and by which all who view it judge its worth. It takes the production process to carry the idea forward—the *muscle* that binds the organism together and gives it strength.

This booklet is a step-by-step review of the book production sequence from manuscript to bound books. The process is not a smooth continuum but rather a series of reminders for a person to stop and look ahead to consider the effect a proper decision in the beginning has on future activities. Some actions can take place concurrently, for example, covers and text might be designed and typeset by two different graphic artists.

Refer to the fold-out chart at the back of this book before reading the text. The heading on each page in the book contains a relevant portion of the production process listed on the chart.

Modern desktop publishing computers and software make it tempting for an author to perform many of the pre-press functions connected with book publishing. Keep in mind the analogy that purchasing a hammer in a hardware store does not make a person a carpenter. This guide will serve its purpose if it instills in an author a basic knowledge of book production enabling that person to talk intelligently to professional designers, editors and artists. An understanding of the entire process from concept to order fulfillment can make workflow more efficient and avert common mistakes that cost time and money. Many of the principles described here apply not only to books but to all printed materials.

This guide refers often to "independent publishers." The term "self-publisher" sometimes carries a stigma in the minds of bookstores, wholesalers and distributors when authors attempt to market their own titles.

Authors may produce manuscripts with either Macintosh or PC-based computers. PC hardware and Windows software has captured the largest percentage of the computer market. However, many graphic designers and printers work with Macintosh.

The most common standard applications for word processing and typesetting—Microsoft Word, WordPerfect, Adobe PageMaker, Quark XPress, Adobe Illustrator, Adobe Photoshop, and Adobe InDesign—are available for both the Macintosh and Windows platforms. Corel Ventura is a page layout program for the Windows platform. An author who submits a manuscript to a designer/compositor or conveys page layouts to a printer must contact the service supplier to be sure that both the platform and the software is compatible and if a particular version of a software application is preferred. A designer/compositor may not yet have converted to the newest versions of all software applications for economic reasons. Also, upgrades to software applications are not always free of bugs which need to be corrected before the new versions become standards in the workplace.

All of these suggestions seem based on the assumption that an author/publisher must be computer literate. Most certainly computers will be used in every stage of book production from word processing through order fulfillment. An author/publisher can work with a designer/compositor who has the required knowledge of computers to ensure efficient handling through the entire production process.

The late Dr. Isaac Asimov was one of the most prolific authors of our time. Dr. Asimov once said, "I'm always writing essays in which I recommend that the whole world be computerized and that everybody work with computers ... and always underneath there is the soft whisper, 'Except me!'" The Isaac Asimov Home Page on the internet states, "Asimov never used a computer to write, only a typewriter, because of personal preference."

Computers and software are always being upgraded. Different suppliers of typesetting, printing and binding have their own personal preferences for equipment and applications that work well for them. The new author/publisher should not be afraid to ask a lot of questions. This advice can be summed up by a Japanese proverb that states, "If you ask a question, you may be embarrassed once, but by not asking you will be embarrassed the rest of your life."

Acknowledgments

The information presented in this booklet is based on the author's personal experience as a production manager for book publishing, owner of a graphic arts studio, and by contact with many fine colleagues in book production and manufacturing for the past forty-five years.

Special thanks to Sharon Tully of Central Plains Book Manufacturing for carefully reading and fine tuning the facts on paper, printing, and binding.

RECENT PLANT TOURS AND CONSULTATION

- American Printing Museum, Los Angeles, California.
- BookMobile, a division of Stanton Publications, St. Paul, Minnesota; Don Leeper.
- Central Plains Book Manufacturing, Winfield, Kansas; Sharon Tully, Jack Fenn, Melody Morris, Günter Hansen.
- Communication Connections, Inc., Phoenix, Arizona; Teresa Kizior.
- Legacy Printing, Minneapolis, Minnesota; Brian Hong.
- Mori Studio, Inc., St. Anthony, Minnesota; Jack Caravela, Jay Monroe, Jaana Bykonich.
- Roswell Bookbinding, Phoenix, Arizona; Jackie Murphy
- Sir Speedy, Scottsdale, Arizona; Mary Dougherty, Shari Bercaw, Mike Bercaw.

PLANT VISITS AND CONSULTATIONS, PAST YEARS

- A.J. Dahl Bookbinding, Minneapolis, Minnesota.
- Banta Corporation, Menasha, Wisconsin.
- Bethany Fellowship Printing Division, Bloomington, Minnesota.
- Colwell Press, Inc., Minneapolis, Minnesota.
- Dahl & Curry Typesetters, Minneapolis, Minnesota.
- Edwards Brothers, Ann Arbor, Michigan.
- Fotocomp Typesetters, Minneapolis, Minnesota.
- Graphtronics, Minneapolis, Minnesota

Acknowledgments

- Heartland Press, Spencer, Iowa.
- Kingsport Press, Kingsport, Tennessee.
- Malloy Lithographing, Ann Arbor, Michigan.
- Mead Papers, paper mill, Chillicothe, Ohio.
- Midwest Editions, bookbinders, Minneapolis, Minnesota.
- Muscle Bound Bindery, Minneapolis, Minnesota.
- North Central Publishing, St. Paul, Minnesota.
- Soldier's Magazine, Pentagon, Washington, DC.
- The Type House, Minneapolis, Minnesota.
- Trademaster Typesetting, Minneapolis, Minnesota.
- U.S. Geological Survey, printing plant, Reston, Virginia.
- Viking Press, Eden Prairie, Minnesota.
- Wausau Papers, paper mill, Wausau, Wisconsin.

WORLD WIDE WEB

The internet proved to be a valuable resource to verify some details and to refresh the author's memory.

No specific web pages or internet addresses are listed here. It is easier to just type a few words in your web browser and search for the information needed. The reader is invited to explore the vast reaches of cyberspace and sort out the useful items.

Although there may be many possible sources displayed for any one search, the author has found that the most helpful references usually appear within the first ten listed.

The author, Morris Lundin, worked as a book designer, layout artist, cover designer and production manager for Burgess Publishing Company, a college book publisher in Minneapolis, for 30 years. He owned a graphic arts business specializing in book design and typesetting for another ten years in Minnesota. He presently publishes several titles under the imprint Mori Studio Southwest in Phoenix.

Costs and Estimates

It is natural for a new author/independent publisher to ask, "How much does it cost to publish a book?" Of course, the answer can vary tremendously. Some experts in the field of independent publishing, suggest that an author should have $5,000 to $10,000 available to spend on all aspects of the production process including a minimum amount of marketing.

"Ballpark" estimates are dangerous. For example, if the ballpark estimate for typesetting a page is "somewhere between ten and fifty dollars," the purchaser will remember the "ten" and the seller will remember the "fifty."

Most estimates of production costs do not take into account the manuscript preparation time by the author. Supposedly, the author/ independent publisher will recap those expenses with profit from the sale of the book.

Copy editing, professional book design, typesetting and layout, printing method, binding method, print quantities, use of color, trim size of the page and shipping distance all affect final cost.

While the manuscript is being written, the author/publisher should jot down specifications for the final book, *i.e.*, projected number of pages, trim size, type of binding and estimated number of copies needed. Request a rough estimate of production costs from specific suppliers or choose a designer/compositor to help. This initial rough estimate will help you determine how to proceed towards a viable product.

Tighter bids should be obtained from three to five suppliers in each category of service as the book project progresses. Estimating is simplified by choosing a supplier that offers the gamut of services from design and typesetting through binding. Convenience does not always mean inexpensive. Complete and accurate specifications must be furnished to the bidders so there are no surprise extra charges after the project is completed.

Printers and binders should be chosen as soon as a manuscript is delivered to the designer. At this time a number of options will be available and decisions made for greater cost effectiveness.

The author/publisher will not always choose the least expensive course through production. Favored trim sizes, cover decoration or binding may be perceived by an author to be more important than cost savings. Cost estimates obtained along the way will give the entire production team a base from which to make choices.

A rough guideline followed by some publishers suggests that a retail price should be from five to nine times manufacturing costs. A series of discounts to retailers, wholesalers and distributors, may amount to 65% of the retail price leaving only 35% for the publisher to cover costs and turn a profit.

The following table indicates the amount of money remaining after discounts on a range of typical retail book prices. The author/publisher can also determine the unit cost necessary to reach a break-even point depending on discounts to bookstores, wholesalers and distributors. Of course, if the author only sells direct to customers, either the unit cost can be higher or the margin of profit greater.

TABLE OF DISCOUNTS AND UNIT COSTS

BOOKSTORE, WHOLESALER, DISTRIBUTOR COMBINED DISCOUNT	SAMPLE RETAIL PRICES					
	$9.95	12.95	14.95	16.95	19.95	24.95
	AMOUNT REMAINING FOR PUBLISHER					
40%	$5.97	7.77	8.97	10.17	11.97	14.97
45%	5.47	7.12	8.22	9.32	10.97	13.27
50%	4.97	6.47	7.47	8.47	9.97	12.48
55%	4.48	5.83	6.73	7.63	8.98	11.23
60%	3.98	5.18	5.98	6.78	7.98	9.98
65%	3.48	4.53	5.23	5.93	6.98	8.73

This table can be used to estimate a break-even retail price by noting how the unit production cost in the shaded area is affected by the discounts in the left hand column. *Remember:* The amount remaining for the publisher must cover all costs of composition, printing and binding, marketing and fulfillment and still provide a profit if the publisher is to remain in business.

Definitions

application — a computer program designed to perform a defined range of functions, *i.e.*, MicrosoftWord for word processing; InDesign, PageMaker or QuarkXPress for page layout; Adobe Photoshop and Adobe Illustrator for handling photos and art.

ASCII — American Standard Code for Information Interchange; letters, numbers, punctuation, etc., set in ASCII can be read by any computer.

basis weight — a system for measuring paper; 500 sheets of the paper's basic sheet size is weighed to determine a basis weight. However, the basic sheet size varies with different kinds of paper.

bleed — any printing that extends beyond the margin and is trimmed off before binding.

book block — interior pages of a book collated in preparation for binding.

brick-and-mortar store — a sales outlet where books are physically present as opposed to internet sales or eBooks.

burn — exposing a photosensitive printing plate to light to transfer an image.

cast-off — an estimate of the number of finished book pages relative to pages of manuscript.

chapter sink — the space at the top of a page containing the chapter title before the text begins.

CIP — Cataloguing in Publication: a process by which the Library of Congress issues a pre-assigned control number for a book.

CMYK — Cyan, Magenta, Yellow, Black: the four colors utilized by offset presses, laser and inkjet printers to create a full spectrum of color; also called process color.

collating (*also* gathering) — placing pages or signatures in proper order prior to binding.

compositor — a person who sets type

creep — when a large number of pages are folded together in a signature or gathered for saddle stitch binding, the center pages protrude further than the outside pages.

crop — to trim down from original size.

dpi — dots per inch: indicates resolution of an image.

dot gain — the amount that a halftone dot increases in size when ink is applied during printing.

DTP — desktop publishing; refers to a configuration of personal computer and laser or inkjet printer used to produce printed materials.

dummy — a sample book made up of blank pages.

dye sublimation — a printing process utilizing solid to gas technology; produces high quality images.

EAN — the Article Numbering system used to produce bar codes for books; consists of ISBN and price. There are 13 digits.

embed — placing art directly in a file's text stream.

EPS — Encapsulated PostScript: a bitmapped graphics file format.

folio — a page number.

font — a single type style; for example, Times Roman, Helvetica.

GBC — plastic comb binding developed by the GBC company.

ghosting — a faint duplicate image of type or art which sometimes appears when printing large areas of color by offset printing.

grain — directional orientation of fibers in paper; in photography, a fine grain presents a clear, sharp image—coarse grain, a rough image.

gutter — inside margin of a page; the binding edge.

guts — the entire contents of a book between the covers.

halftone — dot pattern that makes a photo printable.

hard copy — printed material from computer files or typewriter.

HTML — Hypertext Markup Language; the computer coding used to create Web pages on the Internet.

ISBN — International Standard Book Number: an identification system for books managed by R.R. Bowker.

JPEG — a method for transferring graphic images between computers or applications; developed by Joint Photographic Experts Group; also jpg.

lay-flat binding — any binding that allows a book to open and lay flat on a surface without force; GBC, spiral, plasticoil and Wire-O bindings fit this category; some perfect bound books are specially bound to lay flat.

LCCN — Library of Congress Control Number.

leading — space between lines of type; term originated with hot metal typesetting when lead spacers were inserted between lines of type.

letterpress — printing from an inked raised-type surface

make-ready — preparation of a press for printing.

moire — a secondary pattern of dots formed when two screened images are superimposed one over the other.

OCR — Optical Character Recognition; electronic scanning of text.

offset printing — printing from a plate with a flat surface on which images are burned that will accept an oil-based ink but will repel water. The plate image is transferred to a rubber blanket which, in turn, places the image on paper.

PCN — Preassigned Control Number: issued by the Library of Congress for publishers not eligible for CIP.

PDF — Portable Document Format: a process for converting page layout files by Acrobat Distiller into a uniformly readable digital format.

perfect binding — a paperback book trimmed flush on three sides.

perfecting press — a machine that prints both sides of a sheet in one pass.

pica — a horizontal measurement system for type; there are approximately six picas to one inch.

PMS — Pantone Matching System: a standard for specifying color.

POD — Print-On-Demand: short-run, quick-turnaround printing.

point — a measure of type size, approximately 72 points per inch; also the thickness of cover stock in thousands of an inch.

ppi — pages per inch; used to measure thickness of a book. A page is one side of a sheet, *i.e.*, there are twice as many pages in a book as there are sheets.

recto — a right hand page; odd-numbered page..

register — the process of assuring that colors are printed in their proper places relative to each other.

RGB — Red, Green, Blue: a color system used in inkjet printers; also the default mode when scanning color photos.

RIP — Raster Image Processing: converts PDF files into pages for printing.

RTF — Rich Text Format; ASCII files with special commands to retain fonts, margins, paragraph indents, etc.

running heads — a heading at the top of the page, usually book title on the left page, chapter title on the right page.

self-cover — the first page of a book, containing the title, printed on the same paper stock as the guts of the book with no other cover attached.

signature — a press sheet consisting of 8, 16, 32 or 64 pages when folded; may also be 12, 24 or 48 pages on some equipment.

sizing — a finish applied to the surface of paper to enhance printing quality.

spine — the "backbone" of a book; carries author name, title, publisher logo. May also show ISBN, if room.

spiral binding — pages bound by a continuous metal or plastic wire formed into a coil.

stripping — imposing negatives in proper order on a flat prior to burning an offset plate.

TIFF — Tagged Image File Format: a digitized graphics format.

tracking — adjusting horizontal spacing between letters on a line on type.

trapping — manipulating art and type to overlap slightly for color printing through spreads and chokes.

URL — Uniform Resource Locator; specifies location of documents on the world wide web.

UV — a flow-on protective coating for covers; resin hardens when exposed to ultraviolet light.

verso — a left hand page; even-numbered page.

widow — last line of a paragraph appearing as a single line at the top of the following page; a single first line of a paragraph appearing at the bottom of a page is sometimes called an orphan.

Manuscript Preparation

CONCEPT: TEXT / PHOTOS / ART → **AUTHOR PREP:** COMPUTER: / TYPEWRITER: → COPY EDIT →

The underlying premise of any book project is that it will present information useful to others and give creative satisfaction to the author. Whether a book is a million-seller or a personal edition of 25 copies, careful manuscript preparation is the first step towards presenting a professional product. The independent publisher may be responsible for not only writing text, but obtaining or rendering illustrations and photographs as well.

TEXT

- Browse through books on similar topics in libraries and bookstores, paying attention to trim size, number of pages, use of illustrations/photographs, readability of type font.
- Obtain ISBN from R.R. Bowker. (See Wrap Up, page 75.)
- Obtain permissions from publishers or authors for excerpts taken from previously published material.
- It is not necessary to register a copyright for your material at this stage. Your creation is protected by law until publication. Copyrights are registered after publication and the proper form, two copies of the book, and the registration fee are sent to the U.S. copyright office. (See page 77.)

PHOTOS

- If photos are to be printed black and white, the original glossies should ideally be black and white.
- If photos are to be converted to grayscale from color there should be a distinct contrast between colors and hues.
- Original prints should be larger than, or the same size as, they will appear on the printed page.
- Photo prints should preferably have a glossy finish with a matte finish second choice. Never try to reproduce a photo with a linen finish on the surface.

CONCEPT: TEXT PHOTOS ART → **AUTHOR PREP:** *COMPUTER: TYPEWRITER:* → COPY EDIT →

- Do not reproduce halftone photos from printed pages.
- Search stock photo catalogs for usable images if the photos are to be mainly decorative or of a general illustrative nature.
- Be sure digital photos are high resolution.
- Obtain permissions from publishers or photographers for photos borrowed from previously published material.
- If photos are taken with permission from a publication, request a glossy photo from the original owner.
- Photos designed to bleed should have an image area larger than the essential subject.
- Be sure the main subject in the photo is in the proper proportion to the entire photo. Enlargement of a photo, especially digital photos, will result in an image of lesser quality.
- The main subject of the photo should not be too close to the edge of the photo margin. Leave some room for cropping or straightening.
- Scanned or digital photos should be saved as TIFF on computer and storage media.

ART

- Line illustrations should be rendered in black drawing ink, not pencil or ballpoint pen.
- Illustrations should be prepared larger than, or the same size as, they will appear on the printed page.
- If drawings are for decoration only, check available clip art catalogs or CDs.
- Render art with a line weight that will not be too thin or thick when reduced to final print size.
- Be aware that water color or wash illustrations on textured paper or board will likely show the texture on the printed art.
- Obtain permissions from publishers or authors for illustrations borrowed from previously published material.
- Simple line art may be reproduced with permission directly from a printed page.

CONCEPT: TEXT PHOTOS ART → **AUTHOR PREP:** *COMPUTER:* *TYPEWRITER:* → COPY EDIT →

- Original art should be obtained for illustrations that are to be shaded or screened.
- Utilize a standard application such as Adobe Illustrator, Corel Draw or Adobe Freehand if rendering line art or shaded art.
- Save illustrations as TIFF or EPS computer files if they are to be transferred to designer/compositor on a disk.

AUTHOR PREP: COMPUTER

- Determine whether the Macintosh or Windows platform is acceptable to a designer/compositor.
- If you do not wish to input the manuscript yourself, hire a skilled student or friend. Input by a professional compositor will be more expensive.
- Key-in text utilizing a standard word processing application such as Microsoft Word or WordPerfect.
- An introductory page is a "Foreword" not "Forward."
- A common typographical error is the misuse of "you" and "your" since computer spell checkers will not catch the correct usage. For example, "It is good to see your again," or "We appreciate you business."
- Leave a single word space after each sentence, not two spaces
- Double space between lines for ease in proofreading and marking the manuscript.
- Spell out numbers ten and below.
- Differentiate "0" (zero) and the capital letter "O."
- Use the correct characters for the number "1" and letter lower case "l."
- Do not embed art or photos in the manuscript files.
- Include italics and bold type where appropriate.
- If preparing copy by separate chapters, name the files clearly so a designer can identify sequence easily.
- Save the text often and backup the files at least every day.
- Do not expect art in the manuscript to be placed in exactly the same location relative to text in the printed book.

- Rather than write "...the following figure:..." it is better to assign figure numbers and write, "...as illustrated in Figure 1..."
- Do not manually hard return after the end of each line—let the software program wrap copy.
- Do not manually hyphenate words at the end of lines of manuscript. Use automatic hyphenation or eliminate it altogether.
- Use tab indents for lists rather than the space bar. The amount of indent for tabs need not be set in the word processing stage. The exact indent for each tab will be set by the compositor.
- Do not try to layout word processing text page for page since the type font used in the final design will cause text to flow differently.
- The manuscript does not have to be set in the exact type font that will be used in the printed book.
- Tables and charts set in columns or with rules should be set separately from the main text. Embedded ruled tables often have to be removed from the manuscript and reset by the compositor.

AUTHOR PREP: TYPEWRITER
- Use a typewriter with a black carbon ribbon.
- Be sure the type font does not have broken letters.
- If you do not wish to type the manuscript yourself, hire a student or someone to type the text. Input by a compositor will be more expensive.
- Follow the same rules about spacing, numbers and characters as noted in the instructions for word processing.

COPY EDIT
- Utilize the spell check feature on a word processor for first proofreading.
- Be sure to proofread final copy manually for greater accuracy.
- If your book is to be marketed, hire a professional copy editor to check spelling, grammar and content.

COPYEDITING MARKS

Symbol	Meaning	Example	Symbol	Meaning	Example
lc	lower case capital letter	lower case		insert dash	insert en dash
cap	capitalize letter	capitalize letter		delete	delete
sc	set in small capital letters	set in small caps		close up; delete space	close up
ital	set in italics	set in italics		delete and close up	delete and close
rom	set in roman type	set in roman type	#	insert space	insert space
bf	set in bold type	set in bold type		begin new paragraph	Begin new paragraph
wf	wrong type font; correct it	wrong type font		move right	move right
	insert comma	insert comma please		move left	move left
	insert apostrophe	insert single quote		center	center
	insert quote marks	insert quote marks		move up	move up
	insert period	insert period		move down	move down
	insert question mark	insert question mark		straighten type	straighten type
	insert semicolon	insert semicolon		align vertically	align vertically
	insert colon	insert colon	Tr	transpose	transpose
	insert hyphen	insert hyphen	sp	spell out	sp. out
	insert em dash	insert dash	stet	leave as it was	leave as it was

These are frequently-used copy editor and proofreader marks.

I have a spelling checker,
It came with my PC;
It plainly marks four my revue
Mistakes I cannot sea.

I've run this poem threw it,
I'm sure your please to no,
Its letter perfect in it's weigh,
My checker tolled me sew!

Automatic spell checkers are valuable tools which will catch many typographical errors. However, do not depend on spell checkers alone to catch every misspelling and incorrect word usage.

Author unknown

- If your book is a limited edition book for personal distribution, have a friend who is skilled in language read the manuscript to check spelling and grammar.

REVISE MANUSCRIPT
- Make changes on all word processor files.
- Save only the latest version of a corrected manuscript.
- Retype all pages containing any corrections so the pages will be clean for OCR if page is to be scanned.

EDITORIAL REVIEWS
- Locate authorities in related fields to review non-fiction works.
- Remember that reviewers are potential buyers of the finished book so carefully chosen reviewers can increase your market.
- Endorsements by recognized authors or celebrities can enhance marketability.

FINAL WORD PROCESSING FILES/HARDCOPY/ART
- Save and retain at least one backup copy of the final version of manuscripts prepared on a word processor.
- Furnish electronic files of the final manuscript to designer/compositor on floppy disk, Zip cartridge or CD.
- Always furnish a complete printout (hard copy) of the final manuscript to the designer/compositor.
- Make a marginal notation on each page of the hard copy at the nearest spot where a photo or illustration should be placed.
- Be sure all italics and bolds show up on the hard copy or mark the manuscript carefully to indicate which words or phrases should be so emphasized in the final typesetting.
- Do not embed art or photos in the word processed manuscript. Identify and submit them separately.
- Number or otherwise clearly identify drawings by writing the information in the margin on the front of art boards or on the back.

FINAL WORD PROCESSING FILES / HARDCOPY / ART ⇨ **DESIGN:** *TEXT / COVER:* → DESIGN APPROVAL →

- Number or otherwise identify photos by writing on the backs. NOTE: Be careful not to press hard with a ballpoint pen as it may indent the emulsion on the front of the photo and show up in the final printed book.
- If photos have been scanned or are taken from a digital camera, the disk files should be converted to TIFF rather than JPEG.
- Do not paste final art or photos on the original manuscript or the hard copy furnished.
- All art and photos should be marked numerically or alphabetically.
- If the book is to have an index compiled by the compositor while typesetting, all entries should be marked on the hard copy of the manuscript.
- If the manuscript consists of multiple chapters or exercises, each part must be clearly identified for the designer/compositor. Using an autobiographical book as an example, there are several ways to label chapters. A simple "CH1" and "CH2" would be easier for the compositor to follow if labeled "01 birth" and "02 year 1" if the filename must be restricted to eight characters. Chapters or exercises below the number 10, should be numbered with a preceding zero so they will sort sequentially in a list, *i.e.*, 01, 02, 03, etc.
- Make a xerographic copy of manuscripts prepared on a typewriter and retain in your own files.
- Complete an Advance Book Information (ABI) form for R.R. Bowker to assure the book will be listed in the Books in Print directory. This may be done when the book is far enough along in composition to allow the author/publisher to predict more accurately the publication date.

FACTORS TO CONSIDER WHEN PREPARING A PAGE ESTIMATE

- If every chapter or exercise must begin on a recto page, estimate that there may be a forced blank verso page at the end of half of the chapters in the book.

DESIGN: *TEXT / COVER:* → DESIGN APPROVAL →

- Be sure to allow pages for front matter: title page, copyright page, dedication, table of contents, foreword and preface including any blank verso pages.
- Front matter is usually numbered with lower case roman numerals separately from the body text. Remember to count these pages in the overall number for printing.
- Allow space at the top of each chapter for chapter sink.
- Estimate the space required for illustrations, photos and charts in addition to body text.
- When art is reduced, the size decreases both horizontally and vertically. For example, a narrow illustration reduced to "one-half page" vertically may seem too thin; a wide illustration may take up too little vertical space if reduced to fit the type width.

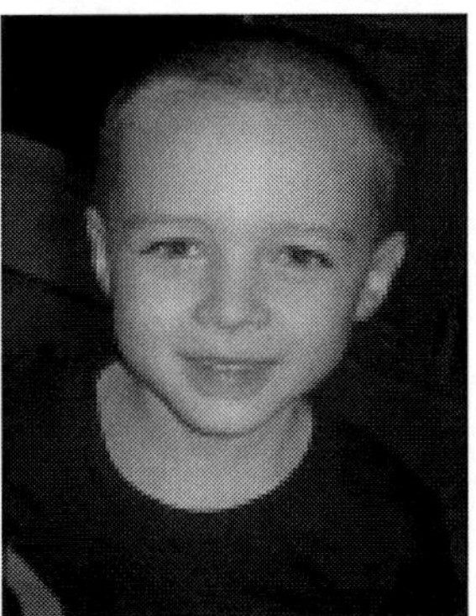 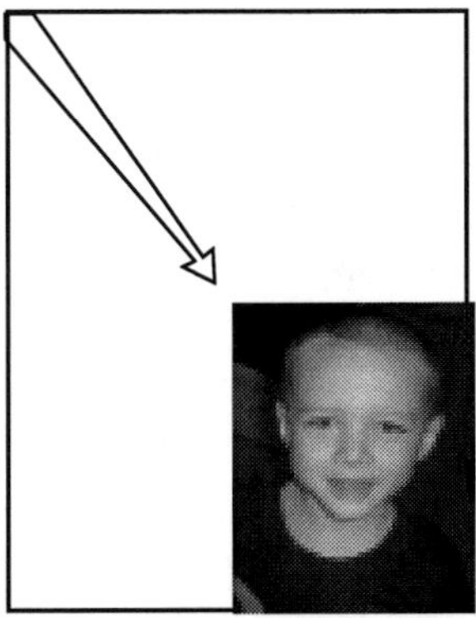

Proportional reduction of art and photos. Note that a 50% reduction in size decreases both the vertical and horizontal dimensions by one-half.

This first estimate should include a projection of number of finished book pages including all art, several print quantities and perhaps several choices of bindings. Estimates should be obtained from three or more designer/compositors, printers and binders. This will aid in planning production and allow the author/publisher to choose a supplier or suppliers.

The following table converts full manuscript pages to final typeset pages in three popular standard book sizes. The estimated pages of solid text must be combined with the factors listed on pages 20–21 to help an author plan the total length of a book.

CONVERTING MANUSCRIPT TO TYPESET PAGES

MANUSCRIPT PAGES* 8½ X 11" Courier type font	FINAL PAGES PER TRIM SIZE		
	5½ X 8½"	6X9"	7½ X 10"
	Times Roman, 12 point on 14 point leading		
50	36	34	25
100	71	67	49
150	107	101	74
200	142	134	98
250	178	168	123
300	213	201	147
350	249	235	172
	Times Roman, 11 point on 13 point leading		
50	31	27	21
100	62	54	42
150	93	81	63
200	124	108	84
250	155	135	105
300	186	162	126
350	217	189	147
400	248	216	168
	Times Roman, 10 point on 12 point leading		
50	27	22	18
100	53	44	36
150	80	66	54
200	106	88	72
250	133	110	90
300	159	132	108
350	186	154	126
400	212	176	144

* Manuscript is based on 12 point Courier type, double space between lines (*i.e.*, 24 point leading), 1" margins all sides.

A manuscript set in 12/24 Helvetica or Arial will carry approximately 26% more copy on the page than Courier type.

A manuscript page of 12/24 Times will carry appoximately 30% more copy on the page.

Design and Composition

Successful book design aids in conveying the intended message without calling attention to itself. With all the type fonts and decorative variations available, it is tempting to use too many in one book. A professional book designer chooses devices to lead a reader smoothly through a book without causing the person to stop to admire the design. Modern desktop publishing technology may give authors of short run books the opportunity to design and typeset their own material. Without the services of a professional designer/compositor, it is more important than ever for the author to observe rules for cost-efficient preparation of book pages for a printer.

DESIGN: TEXT

- The designer/compositor may be asked to do a cast-off in order to request a printing bid.
- A cast-off may help determine a page size that will be more efficient, fit the market preference or most effectively display the subject matter and art.
- A separate cast-off should be made for each page size in question. For example, 100 pages of 8.5 X 11 do not equate to 200 pages 5.5 X 8.5 because of margins and possible use of different type size.
- A quick cast-off may be made by flowing the word processing program file into the page layout file that is set for the final page size including chosen type font and point size. Add to that an estimate of how many more pages the book will expand when art is included.
- Flowing copy into a page layout application is simple if the entire manuscript is in one file. It is more time-consuming if each chapter or exercise is a separate file.

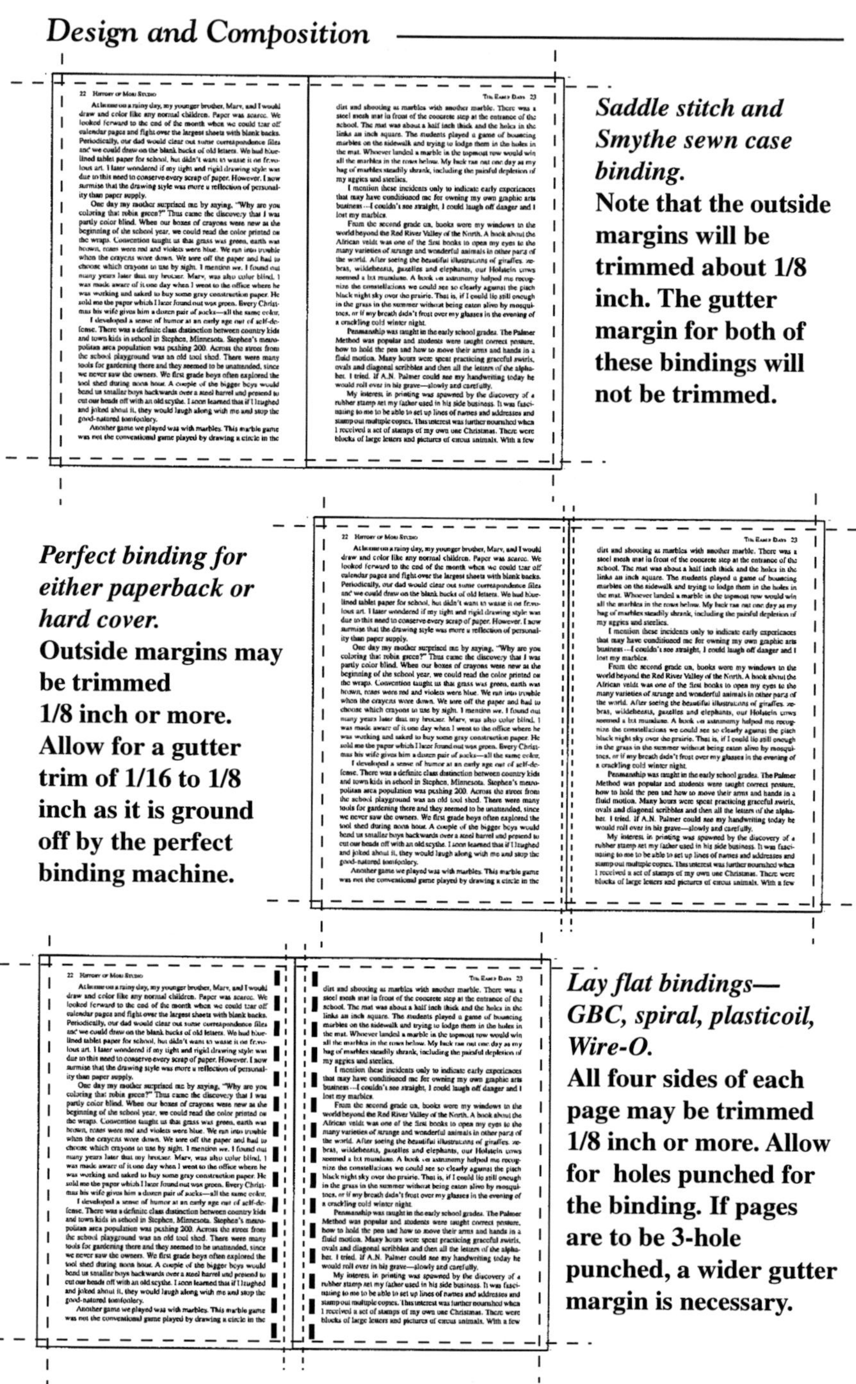

Saddle stitch and Smythe sewn case binding.
Note that the outside margins will be trimmed about 1/8 inch. The gutter margin for both of these bindings will not be trimmed.

Perfect binding for either paperback or hard cover.
Outside margins may be trimmed 1/8 inch or more. Allow for a gutter trim of 1/16 to 1/8 inch as it is ground off by the perfect binding machine.

Lay flat bindings— GBC, spiral, plasticoil, Wire-O.
All four sides of each page may be trimmed 1/8 inch or more. Allow for holes punched for the binding. If pages are to be 3-hole punched, a wider gutter margin is necessary.

Margins and trims on a 5.5 X 8.5 inch page for various bindings.

Type fonts should be chosen for **clarity** and **readability**. There are *thousands* of typefaces available but utilizing more than two or three type styles in a book is distracting.
▶This is COURIER with **bold** and *italics*.

Type fonts should be chosen for **clarity** and **readability**. There are thousands of typefaces available but utilizing more than two or three type styles in a book is distracting.
▶ This is TIMES ROMAN with **bold** and *italics*.

Type fonts should be chosen for **clarity** and **readability**. There are *thousands* of typefaces available but utilizing more than two or three type styles in a book is distracting.
▶This is HELVETICA with **bold** and *italics*.

Type fonts should be chosen for **clarity** and **readability**. There are *thousands* of typefaces available but utilizing more than two or three type styles in a book is distracting.
▶ This is ADOBE GARAMOND with **bold** and *italics*.

Type fonts should be chosen for **clarity** and **readability**. There are *thousands* of typefaces available but utilizing more than two or three type styles in a book is distracting.
▶This is GOUDY OLDSTYLE with **bold** and *italics*.

Type fonts should be chosen for **clarity** and **readability**. There are *thousands* of typefaces available but utilizing more than two or three type styles in a book is distracting.
▶This is GILL SANS with **bold** and *italics*.

These are examples of some common type fonts. Serif or roman type is usually recommended for text. Sans serif or gothic type is used for headings or for short sections of contrasting text. The body of the lower case characters in a font is called the "x" height. The parts of letters extending above the "x" height are called ascenders; the parts dropping below the baseline are called descenders. All of the above fonts are 12 point size.

- Determine printing process and trim size.
- Most common standard trim sizes (inches) are: 5.5 X 8.5, 8.5 X 11, 6 X 9. Depending on the press equipment, other sizes listed by various printers are: 7 X 9, 7.5 X 9, 7 X 10, 7.5 X 10, 9 X 12. Mass market paperbacks may be 4.25 X 7.
- Determine margins according to binding style and trim.
- Choose type fonts for text, headings, captions, quotes, folios, running heads and any other features. For most books, the number of type styles should be limited to two or three type fonts with their respective bold, italics and bold italics.
- Type fonts should be Adobe PostScript or TrueType fonts. Consider the printer's font preferences.
- Text type for books usually ranges from 9 to 12 points.
- Different type fonts or styles vary widely in appearance even though labelled the same point size.
- Decide whether text should be set flush left or justified.
- Plan use of photos and illustrations in layout.
- Prepare several sample page layouts for author approval.
- Include at least one example of each element of design in the sample pages.
- List all "elements of design" on a printed sheet or define styles in the software program's page template.

DESIGN COVER

- Determine method of binding.
- Contact printer for trim size.
- Determine number of colors.
- If one to three colors, choose color from PMS color chart.
- PMS color charts and swatch books are available from art supply stores and sometimes from printers.
- Covers designed for four-color process or digital color printing should be CMYK rather than RGB.
- Obtain photographs or illustrations if required from outside sources.

- Three or more rough designs should be presented for author approval.
- Determine thickness of the book for spine layout after book is typeset and the number of pages known.

TYPESET/LAYOUT: TEXT

- Flow text from word processing program into the page template. If placing text from a word processing application does not work, try copying and pasting.
- Determine the printer's preference for page layout application and version.
- Utilize a standard page layout application such as Quark Xpress or PageMaker. Some printers can also accept material laid out in Framemaker, InDesign or Ventura Publisher.
- The author/publisher should choose a printer/binder by the time typesetting begins.
- Pages must be laid out separately even though displayed on the monitor as facing pages. For example, do not try to lay out two 5.5 X 8.5 inch pages on two halves of a landscaped 8.5 X 11 page.
- Check with the printer to determine if the book will be printed single sheets or in signatures—commonly 8, 16, 32 or 64 pages.
- After determining the signature layout the printer will use, the number of finished pages should fill out complete signatures. Partial signatures will result in higher cost.
- Remember to use PostScript or True Type fonts. Other odd fonts may cause problems when converting to PDF and RIP.
- Do not use multiple master fonts. These may be identified by the initials "MM" following the font name.
- Conventional book layout calls for lower case roman numerals on front matter, *i.e.*, title page, copyright page, preface, foreword or any other material before the first page of text.
- Arabic page numbering begins with the first page of text, usually chapter or exercise one.

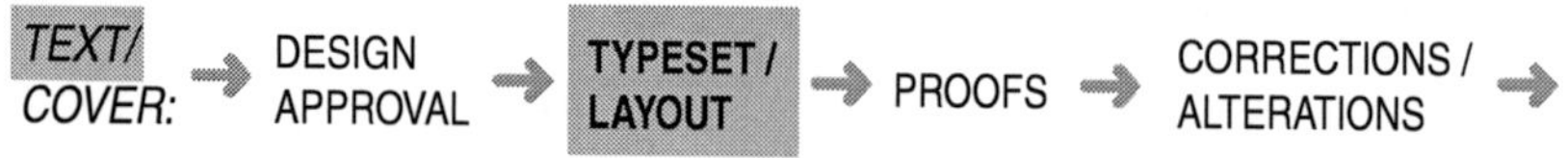

- Some books are numbered consecutively with Arabic numerals beginning with the title page.
- Recto pages are always odd numbers; verso pages are even numbers.
- Decide if each chapter should begin only on a right hand (recto) page or either right or left hand (verso).
- Single word space after sentences.
- Avoid widow and orphan lines.
- Align bottom lines of facing pages if possible.
- Create a list of allowable adjustments to bottom margins, *i.e.*, layout facing pages one line short, rewrite copy, etc.
- Layout applications allow the designer to change leading by fractions of a point, tracking between characters and tweaking the page width by a character or so in order to fit copy to a page. *CAUTION:* If copy is later reflowed, the adjustments may not be consistent between paragraphs on the same page.
- Scan any photos furnished utilizing Photoshop or other application that allows photos to be converted to TIFF. Scanner should be set to 300 dpi before scanning. Changing the resolution setting to 300 dpi after scanning will not improve the quality of the photo.
- Convert any color photos to gray scale after scanning if they are to be printed black and white.
- Some printers recommend that photos or other art be cropped to final proportions in the Illustrator or Photoshop mode before being placed or linked to the pages. This will help reduce the size of page files or linked art.
- Photos and other art should be straightened or squared up in Photoshop before placing in the page layout.
- Digital photos direct from a digital camera usually appear as 72 dpi JPG images by default. The 72 dpi resolution is satisfactory for computer monitor screens, but not for printing.
- Be sure that a photo taken with a digital camera is saved as a 300-line resolution and not the 72-line default.

- Digital photos should be converted to TIFF before placement.
- Photos should be clearly identified for the compositor. Using an autobiographical text as an example, the photos might be numbered thus: "01 mother", "02 father", "03 myface," etc.
- Photos may be placed directly into the layout or linked. Linking photos saves space in the layout.
- If photos are linked, do not change their identification after placing them in the layout.
- Line art or shaded art prepared in Adobe Illustrator or another illustration application should be saved as an EPS or TIFF file before placing in the layout.
- Scanned art should be saved as a TIFF or EPS file before placement in the layout.
- Illustrations should be clearly identified sequentially.
- The illustrations and photos may be numbered and identified in a single sequence or separately. If illustrations are listed separately, they should have a slightly different identification, for example, "A01 streetmap," "A02 house," etc.
- Request a PCN or CIP number from the Library of Congress as soon as the number of pages are known and the publication date is set. The publication date indicates when the book is placed on the market and may be later than the date when all manufacturing is completed. (See page 78.)

LAYOUT: COVER

- Final cover layout cannot be completed until there is an accurate count of the number of pages of text.
- The printer should furnish a paper dummy of the book utilizing the planned paper stock in the exact finish and weight for the cover designer to measure for spine width. In lieu of an actual dummy, the printer may give the information as ppi.
- Type of binding dictates final cover dimensions.
- Art or background color designed to bleed should extend one-fourth inch beyond the trim margins.

- For hard cover books, the binder may furnish a ruled layout as a guideline for the cover designer to follow.
- Avoid breaking a color or illustration at the fold line of the spine on either front or back cover.
- Avoid placing a color strip the exact width of the spine or leaving a white strip the exact width of the spine. Covers can shift slightly during binding and paper stocks can vary in thickness even with the same specifications.
- For covers with two or three PMS flat colors, trapping must be done by the designer/compositor or the printer.
- Avoid placing type closer than one-fourth inch to the outside edges of cover or spine to compensate for any fluctuation in the cover manufacturing and binding.
- The type on the cover spine should read from top to bottom, *i.e.*, if you place the book on a table with the front cover up, the type on the spine should be oriented to read correctly.
- Avoid placing a narrow rule or border around the entire perimeter of the cover as any variation in the trim will cause the margin to be uneven.

The spine type should read from top to bottom. The title and author sequence is often transposed.

When one color is superimposed over another, the colors are *trapped* in order to fit properly. The positive image "S" is *spread* to slightly overlap the negative "S"-shaped *choke* in the background.

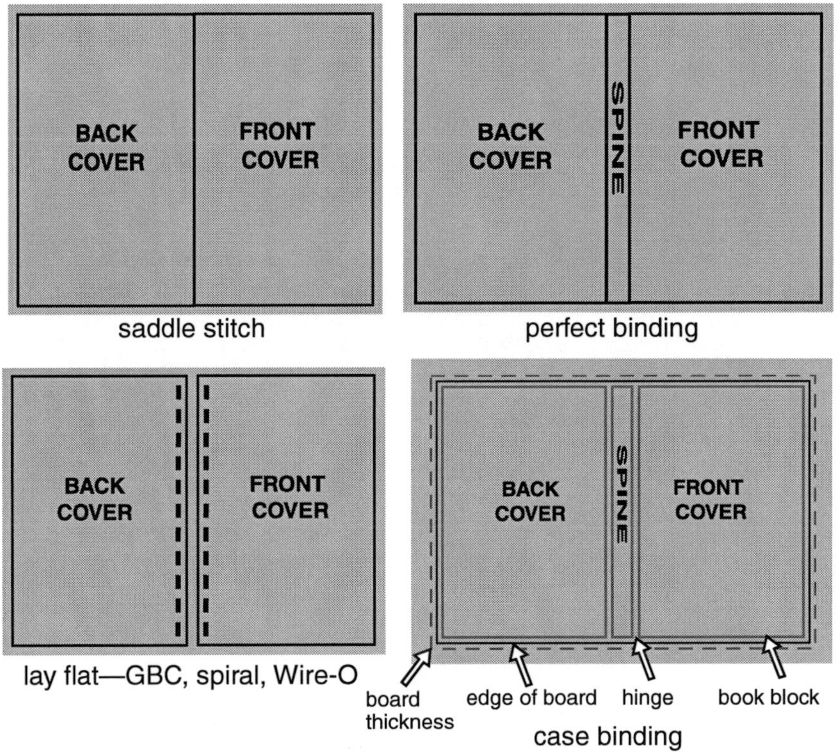

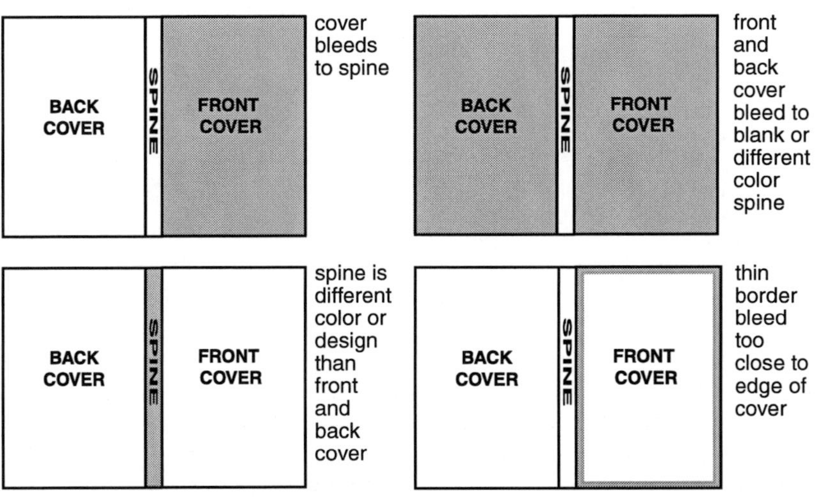

Allowing for bleeds on covers for various types of binding.

Cover designs that can be problematic for printers and binders.

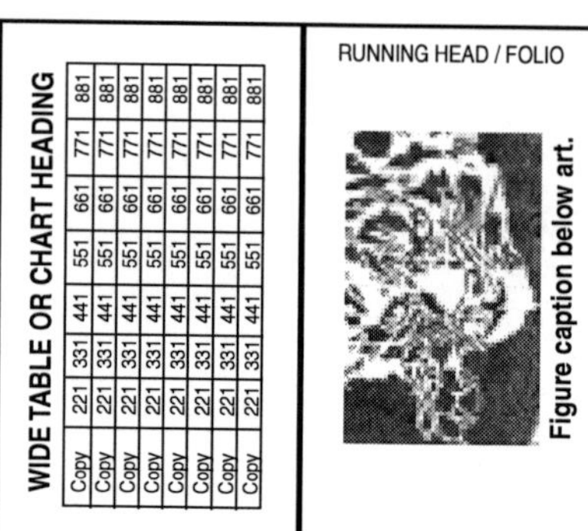

Wide charts or illustrations that must be placed on a page in landscape orientation, should always be readable from left to right on both recto and verso pages.

THIS WAY

NOT THIS

- Compensate for differences in color hues, tones or saturation that may occur between original art or photos and the printed work. Remember that color shown on a computer screen, proofs printed on an inkjet printer, Rainbow proofs from film or digital proofs from PDF files and the final offset- or digitally-printed covers all display color with some variance from each other.
- Complete all versions of the cover design, *i.e.*, both hard cover and paperback if there is to be a split edition. Layout book jacket if required.
- Obtain bar code from a typesetter specializing in bar codes or utilize an application that can set the EAN 13-digit code required for books.
- The bar code contains the ISBN and the price. The numbers 90000 can be set in lieu of a price.
- A separate ISBN and bar code is necessary for new editions of a book as well as each type of binding in an edition.
- R.R. Bowker recommends that the ISBN be printed on the spine of the book. However, a check of books on library or bookstore shelves indicates that this is rarely practiced.
- Plan the entire design package if there are to be both hard cover and soft cover editions or if a book jacket is ordered.
- Plan post cards and bookmarks that might be printed along with the cover run.

Bar codes must be printed in either full height or half height on a book cover. They should not be reduced. This format, EAN-13, is the accepted style for books.
The right portion of the bar code can show the retail price or 90000.
The ISBN is typeset above the bar code but will not be scanned.

TEXT PROOFS

- Proofs of the final layout should be printed out for the author and/or editor to proofread.
- Page proofs are usually printed out on a laser printer. Other printers utilize melted wax and dye sublimation technologies. Inkjet prints are also acceptable if the printing speed and image quality is satisfactory.
- Original manuscript copy should always accompany the page proofs sent to the proofreader.
- The proofreader should mark any typographical errors, punctuation errors, wrong fonts, improper subheads, incorrect placement of illustrations or any other items that do not follow instructions in the original manuscript.
- Proofreader should check for widow lines.
- Proofreader should check for correct pagination.
- Be sure the entries on the Table of Contents match the wording of each chapter or exercise.
- Verify that page references on the Table of Contents match the chapters exactly.

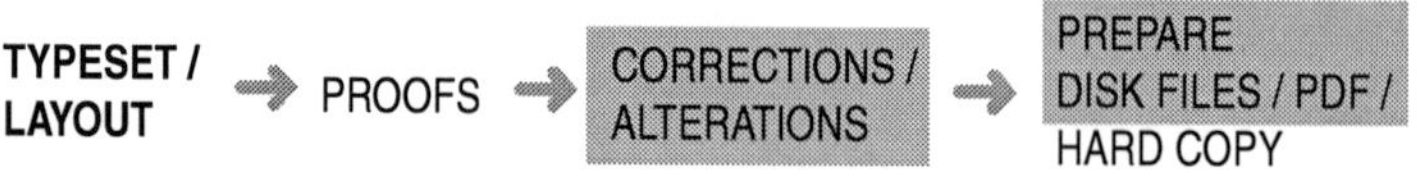

CORRECTIONS/ALTERATIONS

- Corrections made to the pages for items deviating from the original manuscript will not usually be charged for by the compositor. For example, typographical errors, misinterpretation of headings, widow lines, missing copy or erroneous placement of art are the compositor's responsibility.
- Any revisions to text or changes in art requested by the proofreader that deviate from the original manuscript may be chargeable alterations. For example, addition of new text, rearranged sentences, changing sequence of pages, new art added, request for change of fonts, change of margins or page size would all be chargeable.

COVER PROOFS

- Cover proofs are usually printed on an inkjet printer, but may be printed by color laser. Less frequently, dye sublimation or melted wax printers may also be used to provide proofs.
- Remember that colors on an inkjet proof may not appear exactly the same as on a book printed by offset.
- Proofreader should check spelling of title and author's name on cover and spine. Check ISBN, author biography or book summary on back cover, endorsements, bar code and publisher logo.

PREPARE DISK FILES/PDF

- If the printer can accept files directly from the page layout application, *i.e.,* PageMaker or QuarkXpress, be sure to include copies of all type fonts. Also submit all art, even if linked, in a separate file.
- Most printers currently prefer to receive PDF files of both text and cover.
- Convert files to PDF utilizing Acrobat Distiller. Be sure to verify that Distiller settings include embedding all fonts. Be sure photos and art will be transferred at 300 dpi.

TYPESET / LAYOUT → PROOFS → CORRECTIONS / ALTERATIONS → PREPARE DISK FILES / PDF / HARD COPY

- If the book layout contains individual chapters or the front matter is set separately from text, be sure they are numbered in sequence so they will distill in order.
- Verify that color settings are CMYK and not RGB.
- It is not necessary for the designer/compositor to set the screen resolution of halftones. The printer will determine that during RIP preparation for the press.
- After all corrections have been made and pages are complete, the book should be copied to a CD or Zip cartridge for transfer to the printer.
- Other media such as DVDs may be used to transfer data as long as the printer can accept them.
- Most recently, small portable mini storage drives that plug directly into USB ports have been developed that can transfer data from both PC and Macintosh computers.
- A hard copy of the final pages must be furnished to the printer along with the electronic files.
- You may want to furnish customized carton labels to the binder.
- Always copy and retain the final version computer file on disk or file server. For greater security, store a duplicate copy of the final file on a disk in a separate area or building.
- Be sure to store a copy of the page layout files for possible future corrections or revisions and not only the PDF files.
- Remember that PDF files cannot be altered or manipulated.

HARD COPY AS CAMERA READY

- It is possible to furnish the printer a clean laser print to be photographed for offset printing or scanned for digital output. This is called camera-ready copy.
- The output resolution of the copy furnished to the printer should be 600 to 1200 dpi.
- If the trim size is to be less than 8.5 X 11 inches, print out crop marks ("printer's marks") along with the copy on each page.

TYPESET / LAYOUT → PROOFS → CORRECTIONS / ALTERATIONS → PREPARE DISK FILES / PDF / HARD COPY

- For full size 8.5 X 11 inch pages, be sure the text and margins are consistent and exactly as you want them to be placed in the finished book.
- Line art may be printed out in place on the camera-ready pages.
- Low resolution photos (100-line and below) may be pre-screened and either printed out in place on the camera-ready pages or screened separately and pasted down to the page. Screen resolutions above 100 line will probably not reproduce satisfactorily if photographed from a hard copy.
- If glossy photos are submitted to the printer separately, the printer can screen and insert them at considerable additional production cost.

There are several methods for printing books. **Photo offset** is the traditional method of printing larger runs. **Short runs** are produced efficiently by digital printing. The dividing line between digital and offset efficiency can vary. Some printers indicate that *digital printing* is cost effective up to 500 to 800 copies. Other printers can produce books digitally with efficiency up to 1500 copies. Much depends on *page size* and whether pages are printed singly or in multiples.

The original type is a Courier font with some bolds and italics. Note smudge and broken type.

This is a raw scan with no corrections. Compare to the original copy above.

There are several methods for printing books. **Photo offset is the** traditional method of printing larger runs. **Short runs** are produced efficiently by digital printing. The dividing line between digital and offset efficiency can vary. Soi4e printers indic~~,te '--hat digital print!ng is cost effective up to 500 to 800 cQpiq'g. Other printers can produce books cl~liitallv with efficiency ur) tQ 1500 copies.- Much depends on pa,~-e size and whether pages are printed sin,~-"y or -'n multiples.

An example of text scanning by OCR. Type must be clean.

REQUEST FOR ESTIMATE

Name: _______________________ Company: _______________________

Address: _______________________ Email: _______________________

City: _______________________ State: ___________ Zip: ___________

Phone: _______________________ Fax: ___________ Today's Date: ___________

Your CPBM representative: _______________________

Title of Book: _______________________ Est. Print Date : _______________________

1. Final trim size
   - ☐ 5-1/2 x 8-1/2
   - ☐ 6 x 9
   - ☐ 7 x10
   - ☐ 8-1/2 x 11
   - ☐ Other:_______________________

Does inside text bleed?
   - ☐ yes   ☐ no

2. Quantity
   - ☐ 500   ☐ 15,000
   - ☐ 1,000   ☐ 20,000
   - ☐ 3,000   ☐ 25,000
   - ☐ 5,000   ☐ 30,000
   - ☐ 7,500   ☐ 50,000
   - ☐ 10,000   ☐ Other: ———

3. Page Count:_______________________

4. Text provided as:
   - ☐ Camera Ready
   - ☐ Disk to Film
   - Software:_______________________
   - ☐ Mac   ☐ PC
   - ☐ Negatives Provided
   - ☐ Single sheet negatives
   - ☐ Printer spreads

5. Inside text prints:
   - ☐ Black ink throughout (k/k)
   - ☐ Other: _______________________

6. Proofs:
   - ☐ Blueline   ☐ Page Proof
   - ☐ Galley   ☐ Matchprint

7. Text stock
   - ☐ 50# offset
   - ☐ 55# book (bulkier sheet) ☐ cream only
   - ☐ 60# offset
   - ☐ 70# offset
   - ☐ Other: _______________________

8. Number of halftones:_______________________

9. Cover provided as:
   - ☐ Camera Ready
   - ☐ Disk to Film
   - Software:_______________________
   - ☐ Mac   ☐ PC
   - ☐ Composite plate ready film
   - ☐ Matchprint included
   - ☐ Other:_______________________

10. Outside cover prints:
    - ☐ 4/c process
    - ☐ PMS color(s) #:_______________________
    - ☐ Other:_______________________

11. Inside cover prints:
    - ☐ Yes — Color:_______________________
    - ☐ No

12. Cover finish
    - ☐ Gloss lamination
    - ☐ Matte lamination
    - ☐ Gloss varnish
    - ☐ UV coating

13. Cover stock
    - ☐ 10 pt. C1S
    - ☐ 12 pt. C1S
    - ☐ Other: _______________________

14. Binding
    - ☐ Perfect binding
    - ☐ Saddlestitch
    - ☐ Hard (Case) Bound
      - ☐ Adhesive
      - ☐ Smyth-sewn
    - ☐ Other: _______________________

15. Packaging: your books will be bulk packaged in standard sized cartons.
Do you want shrinkwrap?
    - ☐ Yes
    - ☐ Individually
    - ☐ Books per package:_______________________
    - ☐ No shrinkwrapping

16. Books to be shipped to zip code:

____

CPBM will break out the freight charges and show them separately.

17. Method of payment:
    - ☐ Current terms (applicable to established accounts)
    - ☐ 1/2 down with order & 1/2 with return of bluelines

18. Has Central Plains quoted or printed projects for your company in the past?
    - Quoted   ☐ Yes   ☐ No
    - Printed   ☐ Yes   ☐ No

An example of the items that must be covered for an accurate estimate. Courtesy, Central Plains Book Manufacturing, Winfield, Kansas.

When the book is ready for press and the final page count is known, a tighter bid should be obtained from printers and binders. A definite print quantity should be set. If the publisher is not yet committed to one printer or binder, at least three to five estimates should be obtained. Lowest price is not always the criteria for choosing a supplier. Geographic location, turnaround time and fulfillment facilities may be deciding factors.

The following example of jumbled language, which has made the rounds on the internet, seems to contradict all the rules of copyediting.

NOW READ THIS...

Aoccdrnig to rseearch at Cmabrigde Uinervtisy, it deosn't mttaer in waht oredr the ltteers in a wrod are, the olny iprmoetnt tihng is taht the frist and lsat ltteer be at the rghit pclae.

The rset can be a total mses and you can sitll raed wouthit a porbelm.

Tihs is bcuseae the huamn mnid deos not raed ervey lteter by istlef, but the wrod as a wlohe.

Printing

There are several methods for printing books. Offset is the traditional method for printing larger runs. Short runs are produced efficiently by digital printing. The dividing line between digital and offset efficiency can vary. Some printers indicate that digital printing can be cost effective up to 1000 copies. Other printers can produce books digitally with efficiency up to 1500 copies. Some print on demand (POD) suppliers claim to be able to print as few as five copies of a book. However, printing 50 to 100 copies would allow for a more reasonable unit price. Much depends on page size and whether pages are printed singly or in multiples.

Offset books may be printed on either sheet-fed or web presses. The efficiency of make-ready for web presses has brought the minimum run down to 500 to 2000 copies by some suppliers. Again, trim size may be a factor in the decision whether to print on a sheet-fed or web press. The offset image is applied with ink. The color specification standard is the PMS catalog of hues. Full-color printing requires the CYMK series of inks. Each color is applied to the paper separately and in sequence by one of the cylinders on either web or sheet fed presses.

Color printing by offset is costly. A separate film and a plate is needed for each color. The press has to be adjusted to register each color. After this make-ready, the printing speed is essentially the same for one or multiple colors. Web presses print much faster than sheet fed presses. Both sheet fed and web presses currently print faster than digital presses.

The digital press utilizes dry toner xerographic or inkjet technology. Colors available on different machines vary from black only to four colors. Full-color digital printing utilizes the CYMK series of toners. All colors in the xerographic process are applied on one drum and heat-fused to the paper concurrently, thus requiring much smaller equipment that offset. Inkjet equipment sprays liquid ink directly on

LETTERPRESS PRINTING—The type image reads backwards. Ink is applied to the raised surface of the type and the type is pressed directly onto the paper to produce a right-reading image. Letterpress printing from metal type is very rare at present. The Cameron belt press utilizes flexible plastic plates with raised letters attached to two belts which are designed to print one complete book on each pass through the press.

original art

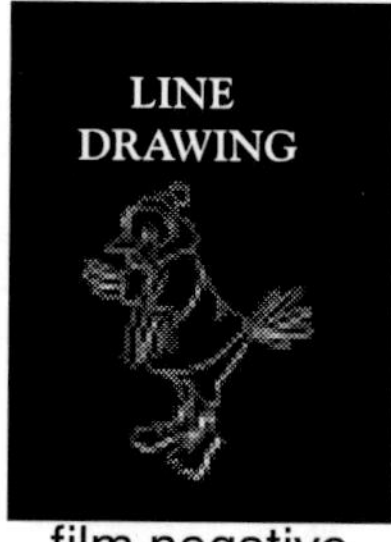

film negative

offset printing plate

OFFSET PRINTING—Type and art is photographed, a film negative made and a metal, plastic or paper plate is burned. The image on the flat surface of the plate is right-reading. Oil-based ink adheres to the image but not to the thin film of water which is applied to the remaining surface of the plate. The image is transferred from plate to paper by a rubber blanket.

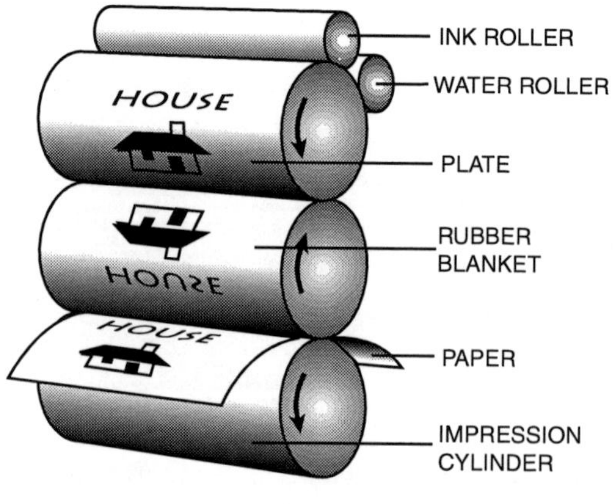

the paper with the resulting mix of four colors producing all hues. Multi-color digital printing does not require the make-ready that is necessary for offset.

Letterpress is very rare except for the Cameron belt press designed mainly to print mass market paperbacks. Type aficionados sometimes print rare manuscripts or art books by letterpress.

CONVENTIONAL OFFSET: CHOOSE PAPER

- All printers have standard paper stocks available that work well on their presses.
- Choosing a printer's standard stock is the most cost effective because the printer orders large quantities of the paper that will run smoothly through the presses.
- Book papers should be selected by weight, opacity, shade, brightness, and finish.
- Grain direction should usually be parallel to the spine.
- Book papers are usually 50# or 60# weight. Paper weights of 70# or 80# may be used to bulk up the thickness of a book or to increase opacity.
- Opacity is determined by thickness, weight and clays added during the paper-making process. Book papers should normally show a 90 or higher reading on the opacity scale. Opacity increases as the numbers increase to 91, 92 and above.
- Brightness of a paper stock is a matter of choice. Very bright white papers register above 85 on a brightness scale.
- Titanium oxide is sometimes added to paper during the manufacturing stage to increase brightness.
- Papers may be coated or uncoated.
  —Uncoated stocks are smooth, vellum and antique.
  —Coated stocks contain clay filler and may be dull or glossy.
- Choice of stock may be influenced by type of textual and illustrative material in the book. Halftones will be cleaner if printed on smooth uncoated or a coated stock. Type-only text may be printed on uncoated antique stock to bulk up a book.

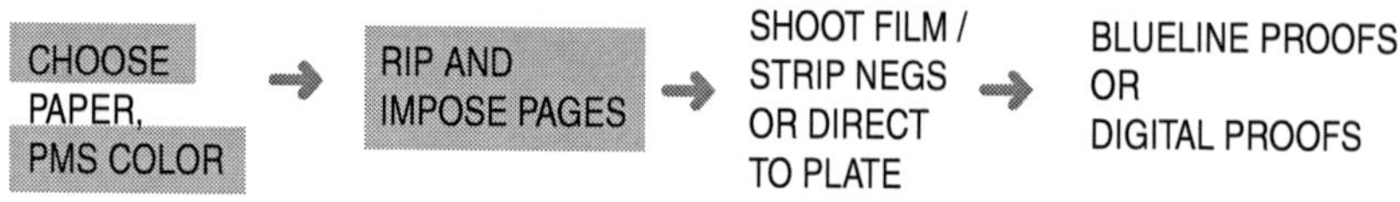

- Cost of paper is a strong consideration especially on large press runs. Paper can comprise 40% to 60% of the printing cost.
- A 50# paper is not necessarily cheaper than 60#. The printer may purchase 60# standard paper in large quantities for substantial savings.

CONVENTIONAL OFFSET: CHOOSE PMS COLOR

- The PMS color system is an industry standard for color.
- Different ink manufacturers may have their own ink swatch books so check with the printer to be sure they can match the standard PMS colors.
- Ink colors need to be specified for one-, two-, or three-color printing projects.
- Four-color process printing utilizes CMYK and no other specification is necessary.
- Be aware that the same ink color will appear different on various kinds of paper. Ask the printer for a drawdown or smear of ink on a paper sample if the color is critical.

RIP AND IMPOSE PAGES

- The preparation of materials prior to actual printing is sometimes called "pre-flight."
- Electronic files received from the designer/compositor must be prepared for page imposition for printing. This process is called "RIPing."
- Books will be printed in signatures of 8, 16, 32 or 64 pages, depending on trim size of the finished book and the press equipment. Signature sizes could also be 12, 24 or 48 pages for some presses.
- The designer/compositor should have checked with the printer to plan the layout for full signatures.
- The signature layout of books printed two-up or double-webbed will be determined by the printer.

HALFTONE SCREENS

Conventional halftone screening of photos consists of breaking up the image into dots of varying sizes to enable printing presses to capture the detail in light and dark areas. This method is also called AM or amplitude modulation screening since the shading depends on the size of the dots. Note that the dots in the areas halfway between white and black are essentially square. Halftones are usually printed at 133 to 150 dots per inch resolution by offset printing. With premium paper and precision presses, 300-line screen halftones are possible. Digital printing, or POD technology, may allow resolutions up to 100 or 120 line screens.

This example for illustrative purposes only. Approximately 16 - 20-lines per inch.

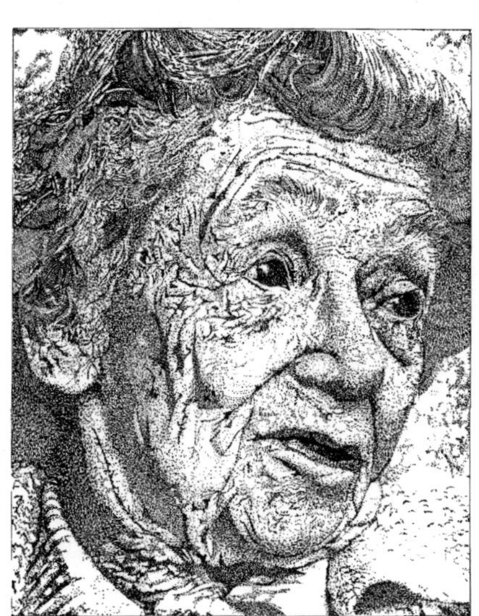

Drawing by Kathy Dalager

Stochastic screening, developed in the mid-90s, is also called FM or frequency modulation screening. The image is made up of many small dots all the same size. The shading is created by number of dots in a given area.

Stochastic screening is said to give a high-quality image even on uncoated stock. It has not yet been widely used because it requires more meticulous plate prep technology than conventional halftones.

This example is not a stochastic screen but rather a stipple drawing to illustrate the process.

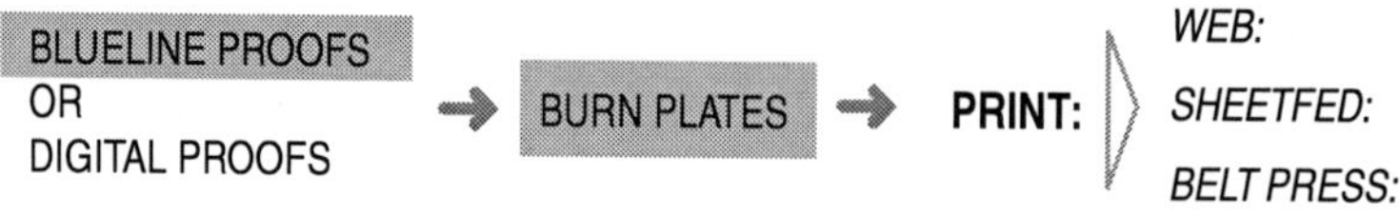

- If film negatives and metal plates are to be used for printing, pages will be shot individually or in partial imposition.
- Film may be stripped manually into forms or positioned electronically by Opticopy equipment.
- The stripper places the film on a light table and checks for pinholes in the emulsion. These holes are opaqued with a small brush and thick paint.

BLUELINE PROOFS

- Once the film is imposed in signature form, blueline proofs are made for the designer/compositor and/or author to proof. These proofs are sometimes called Dylux proofs or silverprints.
- At this stage, there should be no changes to typeset copy.
- Check for correct sequence of signatures.
- Check for correct page sequence.
- Check alignment of running heads and folios.
- Check for correct margins.
- Check for "clean" pages, *i.e.*, mark any extraneous specks that might appear due to tiny holes in the negatives.
- Check for any breaks in the type caused by slivers of material on the negatives.
- Mark any corrections clearly, preferably with red marker.
- Mark and sign or initial the proofs with "OK" or "OK with corrections."
- Check the ISBN one last time.

BURNING PLATES

- The negatives are placed in a vacuum frame, film emulsion in contact with the photosensitive emulsion on a metal plate.
- Film may also be used to burn plastic or paper plates.
- After exposure to light, the plates are developed and made ready for the press.

DIRECT TO PLATE/DIGITAL PROOFS

- The RIP (raster image processor) arranges the pages in signature form.
- After imposition, a proof is printed out on a digital printer.
- More efficiency and cost savings are attained by eliminating the film and exposing pages directly to plates.
- Pages burned direct to plate will often be on mylar or paper plates rather than metal.
- The designer/compositor and/or author should follow the same steps for proofing as with bluelines.
- After proofs are approved or corrected, the photosensitive plastic or paper plates are exposed to light, developed and prepared for press.
- Signatures are folded and collated the same as blueline proofs.

PRINTING: WEB PRESS

- Web printing means that the paper is fed through the press from continuous rolls (webs) hung on one end of the machine.
- Number of pages in a signature is determined by trim size and press sheet size.
- The paper passes through the press only once and both front and back of the sheet is printed. All web presses are perfecting presses.
- The number of colors that can be printed is determined by the number of inking stacks on a press. Printing from one to eight colors is possible depending on the printing equipment.
- The web of paper is cut and folded into signatures inline at the end of the press.
- For other than case-bound books, the signatures are usually perforated on the press to facilitate accurate folding.
- For Smythe sewn books, the binding edges of the signatures cannot be perforated.
- A book printed on a four-color press utilizing only one or two colors may be double-webbed. The two webs merge before fold-

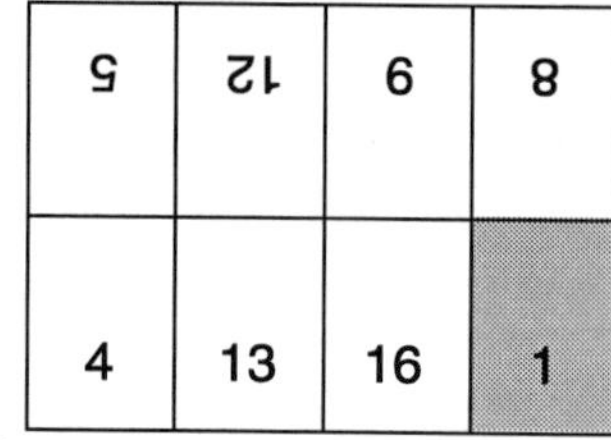

Front

Back

Layout diagram of a 16-page signature. Note orientation of the pages as represented by the numbers. This would be one of the smallest signatures for book printing. Most books are printed as 32-pagers. Smaller trim size books might be printed in 64-page signatures if the paper weight is light enough to facilitate accurate folding and the press sheet is large enough.

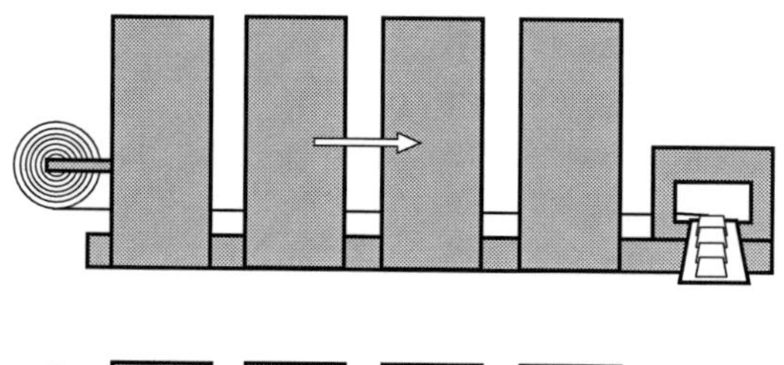

The web press at left represents one web being printed four color, two sides, on a single pass through the press.

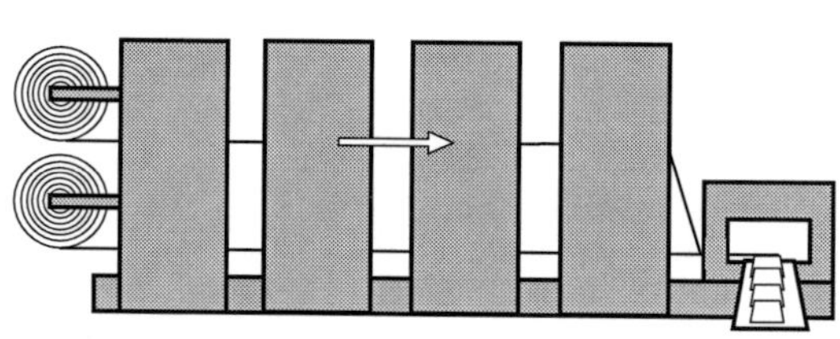

The second diagram illustrates how two webs may be printed two colors, two sides, on a single pass through a four-color press.

This is a simplified diagram of a two-color sheetfed press. The sheetfed press may print one or both sides of a sheet at a time. Presses printing both sides of a sheet on one pass through the press are called perfecters.

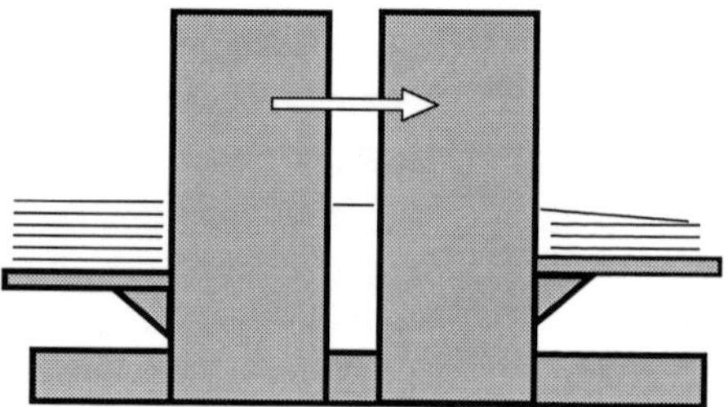

Simplified diagrams of web and sheetfed presses.

PRINT:	WEB:	PRINT SIGS / FOLD ON PRESS / PERFORATE
	SHEETFED:	PRINT / PERFORATE SIGS ➡ FOLD
	BELT PRESS:	ONE PASS PRINT, FOLD, COLLATE ENTIRE BOOK

ing and result in a signature containing twice the number of pages as a single web.

- The folded signature dimension is larger than the finished book size to allow for trim after collating.
- Signatures are collated on a separate machine, usually the perfect binder.

SHEET FED PRESS

- The sheet fed process means that one large sheet of paper at a time passes through the machine from a stack of sheets on one end of the press.
- Sheets may be printed on one side at a time or both sides on a perfecting press.
- Sheet fed presses exist that can print one, two, four, five, six or eight colors.
- Four-color process can be printed on a two-color press. After two colors are printed, the plates are replaced for the remaining two colors, the ink fountains washed-up and filled with new ink.
- Printing four colors on a two-color press requires a stable paper stock. Temperature and humidity must be controlled in the pressroom to avoid distortion of the paper between runs.
- The same make-ready procedure is required for multiple colors on sheet fed presses as on web presses.
- Signatures are folded on a separate machine.
- Perforations are normally made by notched perforation wheels on the folder. Perforation tapes can also be adhered to offset press plates.
- For saddle stitch, spiral, GBC and Wire-O binding, the signatures are collated before binding.
- For perfect binding, the signatures may be collated inline on the binding machine.
- Collating and unique steps for Smyth sewn case bound or hard cover books are described in the binding section.

	WEB:	PRINT SIGS / FOLD ON PRESS / PERFORATE
PRINT:	*SHEETFED:*	PRINT / PERFORATE SIGS ➡ FOLD
	BELT PRESS:	ONE PASS PRINT, FOLD, COLLATE ENTIRE BOOK

GENERAL

- The printer usually orders more paper than necessary for an exact quantity to allow for spoilage.
- The quantity of each signature can vary due to press problems with an individual signature, paper spoilage or damage while folding or collating.
- Insisting on delivery of an exact quantity without underruns or overruns may result in a higher price because the printer has to order excess paper to be certain there are no shortages. This requirement may also result in extra copies being thrown away.
- Approximately five to ten per cent of paper can be consumed in the make-ready stage as registration and ink coverage is adjusted.
- Multiple-color printing consumes more paper during make-ready than a one-color job.
- Web presses, because of their speed, generally consume more paper during make-ready than sheet fed presses.
- Industry standards state that the delivery of the quantity of books ordered, plus or minus ten percent, is deemed to be acceptable.

BELT PRESS

- The Cameron belt press is available at a select few printing companies in this country.
- The belt press is a web-fed letter press.
- Flexible plastic page-sized plates are fastened to two continuous belts with adhesive. Each belt prints one side of the web.
- The press is designed to print, fold and collate an entire book block in one pass through the press.
- Usually a perfect binder is placed inline with the press resulting in the manufacture of complete books in one operation.
- The press is designed for efficient printing of mass market paperback books with mainly typeset copy.
- The press may print line art satisfactorily but only low-resolution halftones are possible.

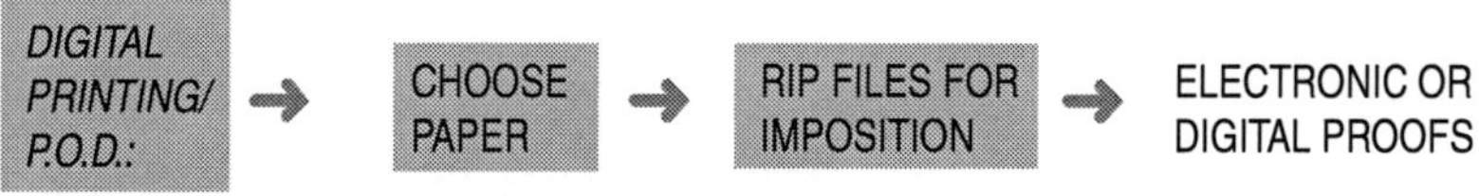

OTHER PRINTING METHODS

- Some huge quantity periodicals may be printed by rotogravure but this would be rare for book printing.
- Some cover designs may be printed by silk screen.
- Letterpress equipment may still be used for die-cutting and serial numbering.

PRINTING: DIGITAL/POD

- Digital printing applies to laser, xerographic or inkjet processes.
- Digital printing technology has created a POD industry geared to printing short runs of books with short turnaround time.
- Printers utilizing digital presses prefer to receive material as PDF files.
- Be sure to check all PDF output carefully to be sure the pages match the final layout and all fonts and illustrations are embedded correctly.
- Files can be transmitted over the internet or delivered on CD or Zip cartridges. DSL or Broadband lines provide faster transmission allowing larger files to be sent.
- Even though smaller electronic files can be sent over the internet, most printers still insist on receiving a hard copy of the pages from the designer/compositor.
- Page layout files received on disk or electronically are RIPed to prepare them for printing.
- Halftone screen frequency of dots per inch is set when RIPing. Ask for an example of screen reproduction. Usually photos reproduce best at 85 lines to 100 lines per inch.
- Because of the short run, it is most economical to choose the printer's standard 50# or 60# paper stock.
- Since many books are printed in single sheets, planning page count to fit signatures is usually not an issue.

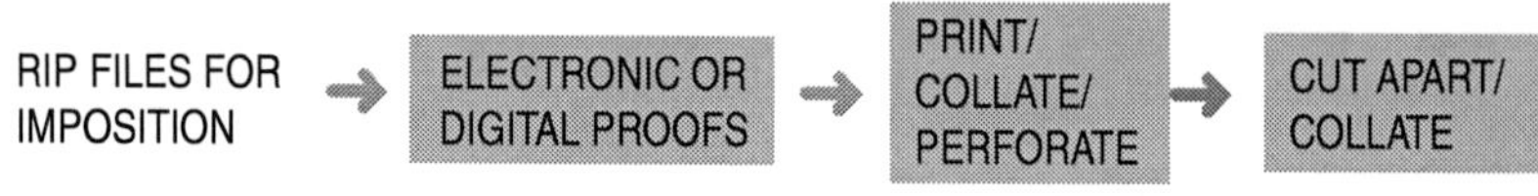

ELECTRONIC OR DIGITAL PROOFS

- After the files are RIPed, proofs may be sent electronically over the internet to the designer/compositor and/or author.
- Pages will most likely be proofread on the computer monitor. A printout on your laser printer does not guarantee that copy will look the same as the final digital print.
- Check for correct page sequence.
- Check for any missing art or photos.
- Phone, e-mail or fax the corrections to the printer.
- If a digital printout is furnished for proof, check for page sequence and missing art or photos and clearly mark corrections on the pages. Fax or mail marked-up pages to the printer.

PRINT/COLLATE/PERFORATE/CUT APART

- Digital printing is generally feasible for runs from 25 to 1000 copies. Some printers claim to be able to print as few as five copies or as many as 1500 copies economically.
- Xerographic digital presses offer 600 dpi resolution.
- Standard sizes are 5.5 X 8.5, 8.5 X 11 and 6 X 9.
- Pages may be printed to any size within the 8.5 X 11, but odd-sized pages will result in waste of paper and lost efficiency.
- Economical printing of runs up to 1500 copies is achieved if the trim size of the book is small enough to allow two to four pages to be printed at a time on one sheet.
- Multiple pages are usually printed duplex and cut apart.
- If the book is to be saddle stitched, the pages must be printed in a minimum of four-page signatures.
- The Xerox Docutech was the first xerographic production line machine. Some other manufacturers entering the field are Toshiba, Canon and Heidelberg.
- Some digital presses can print duplex, collate and staple a booklet in one pass through the machine.
- Workbooks or looseleaf material requiring a 3-hole punch can be printed on pre-drilled paper stock.

Comparative Workflow of Traditional Offset vs. Digital Printing

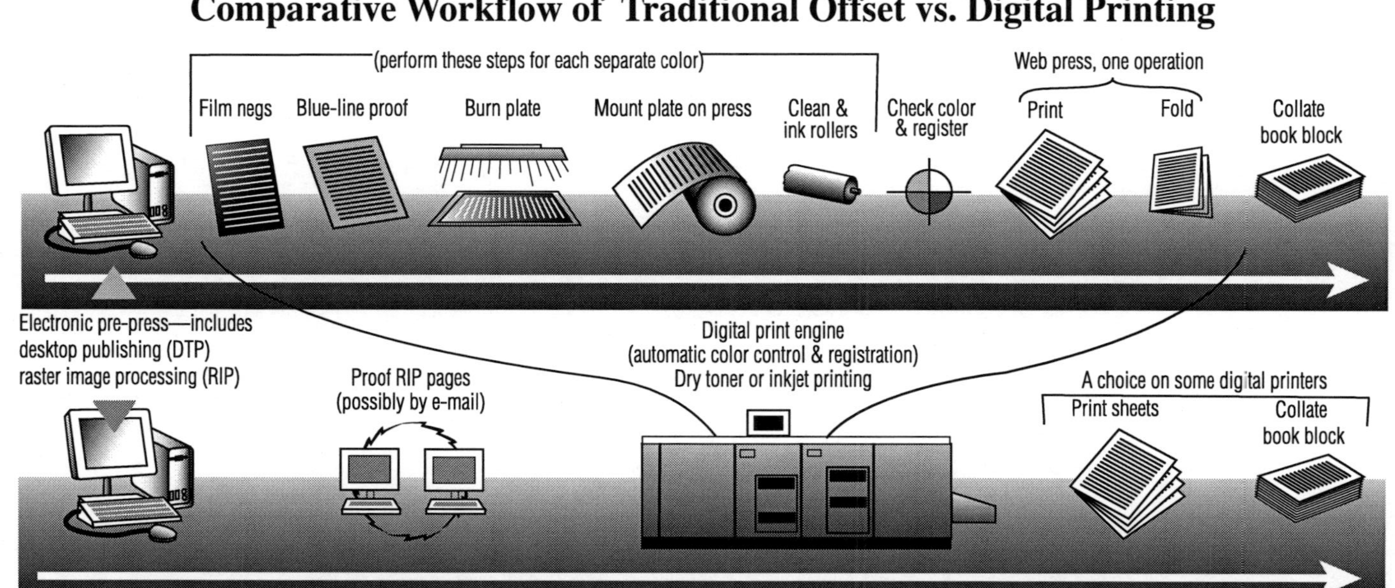

Diagram modified from art furnished by Mary Dougherty, Sir Speedy, Scottsdale.

Digital equipment is quicker and simpler to make-ready than offset. Digital printing machines run slower and handle smaller sheets of paper than offset presses. Larger print runs are produced more economically by offset. Books printed in only one color require just one set of negatives and plates, so the cost difference between offset and digital production may be minimal for medium runs. Durability of the digitally printed image using toner powder or inkjet ink versus offset ink has not yet been reliably determined.

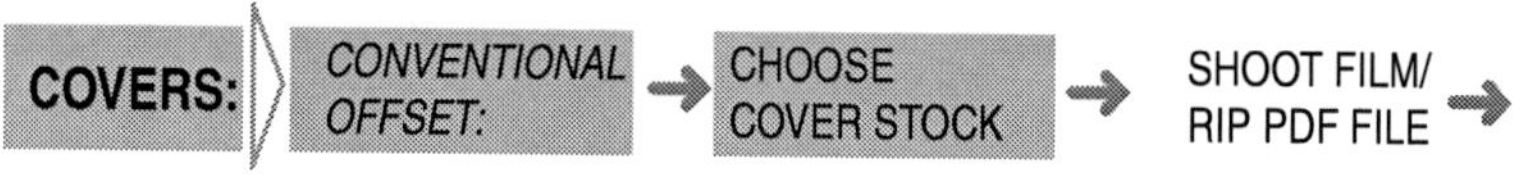

- Booklets may also be 3-hole drilled after collating before the covers are assembled to avoid drilling covers after binding.

COVERS: CONVENTIONAL OFFSET

- Printers prefer to receive PDF files.
- Printer may be able to accept files in page layout applications such as PageMaker or QuarkXpress without conversion to PDF.
- Camera-ready copy may be furnished with overlays for second or third colors. This method has largely been replaced by electronic files.
- The designer/compositor needs to allow 1/4 to 1/2-inch bleed beyond the trim size of the bound book.
- Most covers are printed on sheet fed presses.
- Covers may be scored to fold accurately on both sides of the spine. This is especially important if covers fold cross-grain.
- If camera-ready art (reflective copy) is provided, the printer will shoot film for each color.
- Cover stocks may be uncoated or coated stock.
- Cover stock may be coated one or both sides.
- Coated stock may be matte, dull or gloss finish.
- A slurry of clay is applied to the paper stock at the mill by doctor blade or drum. Drum coating creates a higher gloss.
- Glossy stock should be used for the best ink holdout even if covers are to be laminated after printing.
- Cover stock is specified by basis weight. However, a 65# or 80# cover weight is different than a 65# or 80# text weight.
- The most popular cover stocks are 10 point or 12 point coated one side, matte finish. The lightest weight cover stock could be 8 point, equivalent to 100# offset.
- PDF or page layout files are RIPed for imposition on plates before creating film.

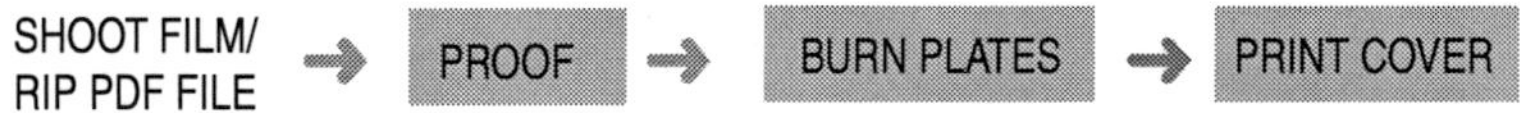

PROOF

- A color proof is made to show colors as converted from PDF.
- Designer/compositor and/or author must check to be sure all elements of the design are complete.
- Check spelling on title, subtitle, author(s) name, back cover copy.
- Check publisher's logo, ISBN and bar code.
- Several methods of proofing produce different kinds of proof.
- Proof processes that do not use the same paper and ink as the actual press run are not absolutely accurate.
- Matchprint and Chromalin are two film laminate proofs that are accurate enough for color check.
- Iris prints are high quality inkjet prints that could be used for close color match.
- Dye sublimation printers produce high quality prints that can be used for close color match.

BURN PLATES

- Postcards or bookmarks may be stripped into the final film if there is room around the main image on a sheet.
- Final film is contacted to photosensitive metal plates in a vacuum frame, exposed to light and developed.

PRINT COVER

- Most covers will be printed on a sheet fed press.
- Depending on the size of the cover and the cover stock the press can accommodate, covers might be printed in multiples.
- Covers may be printed on one- or two-color offset presses if the design calls for a minimum of colors.
- Four-color process covers are more efficiently printed by one pass through a four-color press.
- Even after all the pre-press color checks have been made, the press operator's preferences can be a factor in running color.

- Checking the color bars printed in the margins of the press sheet with a spectrophotometer will assure the most accurate color throughout a pressrun.
- The operator also checks for trapping and dot gain if flat PMS colors are used as well as for four-color process.
- For four-color process jobs, the operator checks for color density, dot gain and screen angles.
- The press operator should watch for ghosting, especially on covers with type reversed out of large areas of solid ink.
- Ancillary materials may be cut away from the cover by the printer before delivering to the book binder.
- The binder may prefer to trim off appended items to assure there is sufficient room left on the cover for proper binding.
- The printed spine should be centered on the sheet for covers that are to be perfect bound.
- Check with the binder to be sure there is enough bleed and a lip for perfect binding.
- For saddle-stitched covers the fold should be centered on the printed sheet.
- For spiral, plasticoil and GBC covers, either the printer or binder will trim the front and back covers separately to the proper size before collating.

COVERS: DIGITAL/ELECTRONIC OR DIGITAL PROOF

- Cover stocks may be coated or uncoated.
- Printers stock paper in the most frequently-used standard sizes. Odd sizes requiring special order will normally be more expensive.
- The cover stock for digital printing may have a special surface sizing to accommodate inkjet inks or xerographic toner.
- Cover weights are normally 10 point or 12 point.
- Printer RIPs the PDF file furnished by designer/compositor.

- Files may be sent over the internet to designer/compositor and/ or author for proof.
- Proof files received over the internet are not suitable for accurately checking color since they would default to the monitor's range of colors.
- Printing out a proof on an inkjet printer at home would not be a true test of color since the printer's equipment is different.
- The printer may output the cover on a digital printer for proof which would allow the most accurate assessment of color.
- Check to be sure all elements of the cover design RIPed correctly, *i.e.*, title, subtitle, author name(s), publisher logo, barcode, back cover text and spine.
- Be sure to communicate cover proof OK or OK with corrections to the printer by e-mail, phone or by marking directly on a printout and mailing.

PRINT

- Digital presses may not handle as large a sheet of cover stock as a sheet-fed offset press.
- Check with printer to see if there is room on a cover sheet for postcards or bookmarks.
- All colors print on one pass through the press so registration should not be a problem.
- Digital printing is very efficient for producing short runs of full-color covers.
- Digital press may not print as many pages per minute as offset presses but makeready time is much shorter.
- A cover might be printed on a digital press even though the book's text is printed by traditional offset.
- Digitally printed covers might be personalized, *i.e.*, change imprints for a specific market or customer.

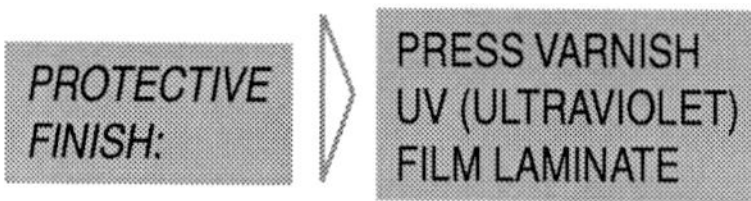

PROTECTIVE FINISH

- The same protective finishes may be applied to offset or digitally-printed covers.
- Press varnish is a liquid coating that is applied to the cover on an offset press after the colors are printed.
- The varnish may be applied on the same pass through the press if the press has one stack of cylinders more than the number of colors printed. Usually the varnish would be applied from the fifth stack of cylinders on a five-color press.
- Press varnish could be applied to a digitally-printed cover but would be an additional press run on an offset press.
- Varnish is the least expensive coating and least durable.
- UV coating, sometimes called flow or flood coating, is more durable and more expensive than press varnish.
- A special resin is applied to the printed cover as a liquid and exposed to ultraviolet light to harden.
- UV coatings may be applied inline at the end of the press or on a separate machine.
- Color tints may be added to varnish coating for special effects.
- Spot varnish may be applied to specific areas of a cover or other printed page on coated stock. This requires a burned offset plate the same as an additional color.
- Varnish or UV coatings can be either glossy or matte finish.
- Cleaning the press fountains after using varnish is one of the least favorite activities of a press operator.
- Film lamination is the most durable, most expensive and probably the most popular method of coating.
- Thin polyester film is supplied with a heat-sensitive adhesive backing that will adhere to the cover.
- Various thickness combinations of polyester and adhesive are available. A common thickness would be .005 of an inch.
- Film laminates may be either glossy or matte.

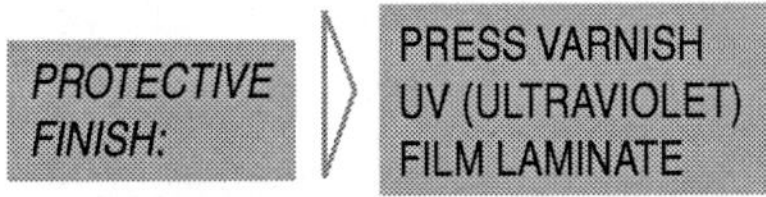

- With the adhesive side of the film laminate facing the outside of the printed cover, the two sheets are passed through rollers to adhere the film to the cover with heat and pressure.
- Laminates adhere well to uncoated or matte finish coated stock as well as to the standard 10 point coated-one-side stocks.
- This process bonds a material which is impervious to moisture to the outside of a cover stock while the uncoated inside of the cover can absorb moisture.
- The uneven absorption of moisture and wrong grain direction can combine to cause a cover to curl.
- Request the printer to furnish lay-flat lamination to help avoid the curl problem.
- Consult the printer to choose the best thickness of lamination film in relation to the cover weight.

Binding

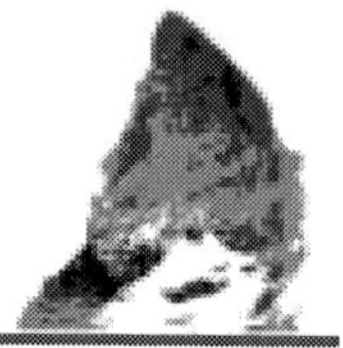

Choosing the proper binding begins with an analysis of the end use and customer preference. Books likely to be part of a library collection should preferrably be case bound. Novels or non-fiction books for the general market are usually perfect bound paperbacks. Workbooks and manuals might be more convenient for consumer use if spiral, Wire-O or GBC bound. Smaller instruction booklets or teacher's guides would be more economically bound by saddle stitching.

Preparation for the binding begins with the designer/compositor. Margins have to be set to take into account the amount of paper trimmed by the perfect binder. The number of text pages might suggest one type of binding over another. Cover layouts are directly related to the type of binding planned.

Saddle stitching is the least expensive binding. Perfect binding is normally more economical than the lay flat bindings—GBC, Wire-O, spiral or plasticoil. Relative costs may be determined by which equipment a printer has in house. Case binding or hard binding is the most expensive and considered the most durable.

Some processes are not sharply defined between printing and binding. For example, folding signatures and collating could be performed during either the printing or binding process.

SADDLE STITCH

- Saddle-stitch binding is where the booklet is folded in half and two or three staples are punched through the center of the fold to hold the pages together.
- Grain direction should be parallel to the spine if at all possible.
- Covers that are heavy weight or printed with grain crosswise must be scored on the fold line before binding.

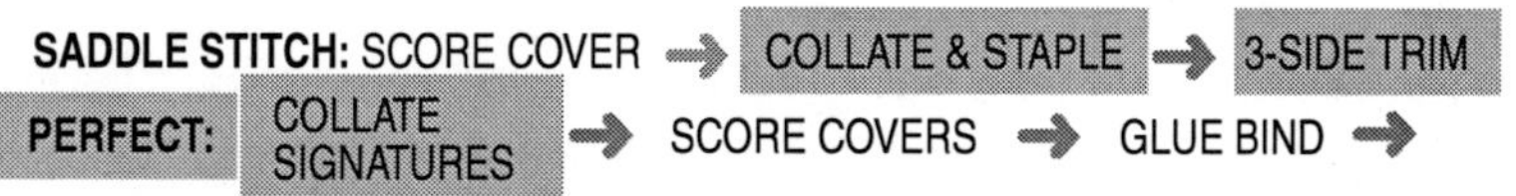

- Saddle-stitch binding is usually limited to books of not more than 80 pages depending on weight of paper stock. Some binders set the minimum at 100 pages.
- Signatures of 8, 16 or 32 pages can be saddle stitched. Four-page signatures are the minimum required.
- The signature layout is different than other binding processes so the printer needs to plan the signatures to nest one over the other rather than stack.
- Signatures to be saddle stitched cannot be perforated on the binding edge.
- There is no spine on which to print title and author's name so this type of binding would not be satisfactory for books that are to be displayed in a library.
- Standard 10 point and 12 point cover stocks are acceptable.
- There are many colored paper stocks available. Use of a colored stock and one-color printing can result in an attractive but economical cover.
- The designer/compositor does not need to allow for trim on the gutter margin of the pages.
- The designer/compositor neeeds to allow for a certain amount of creep on the trim margin.
- Saddle stitched books are trimmed on three sides after being stapled.
- The trim size of a book may be slightly less than specifications, *i.e.*, an 8.5 X 11 book may end up at 8-3/8 X 10-3/4 inches if there is no room for bleed or trim on the press sheet.

PERFECT BINDING

- Perfect binding is also referred to as paperback.
- Perfect binding is so called because it is trimmed perfectly flush with the cover on three sides.
- Printed signatures can be perforated along top and spine before collating for perfect bound books.
- Many binders prefer perforated signatures to let trapped air escape during folding resulting in more accurate folds.

PERFECT: COLLATE SIGNATURES → SCORE COVERS → GLUE BIND → 3-SIDE TRIM

- Folded signatures may be collated before running through a perfect binder or may be collated inline depending on the binding company's equipment.
- Designer/compositor should allow for 1/8 inch to be trimmed off the gutter edge of the signatures and set the margin of the page accordingly.
- The binding equipment must saw or grind the folded spine to expose all pages to the glue before attaching the cover.
- The printed design on the cover should be large enough to allow a 1/8 to 1/4 inch trim off three sides in addition to the amount sawed off the spine.
- If the book contains a small signature, *i.e.*, an 8-page signature among 32-page signatures, the small signature should be placed toward middle of the book rather than face either front or back cover.
- Perfect binding is suitable for a minimum of 48 to 64 pages depending on paper stock. Spine cannot be less than 1/8 inch.
- The spine of the cover should be about 1/4 inch longer at the head than the collated signatures in order to trap excess glue from the binding machine.
- Cover stock is normally 10 point or 12 point. Lighter weight cover stocks can wrinkle during the binding process.
- Thin books should have light weight (8 point) cover stock.
- Covers will most likely be scored on each side of the spine to facilitate accurate folding around the book.
- Grain direction of the cover stock should be parallel with the spine if at all possible.
- The gutter or spine side of a signature is sawed or ground off to expose all sheets and to provide a rough edge for glue penetration.
- Uncoated printing paper generally allows a stronger bond with the glue than coated paper.

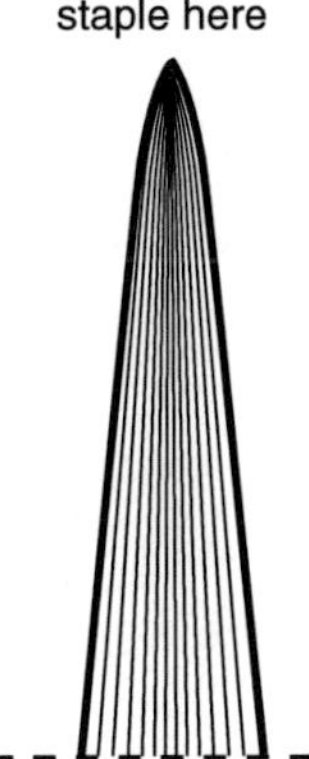

Saddle stitch, **top view. The more pages in the book, the further the pages protrude on the front (creep). For books with 64 pages or more, the designer/ compositor may have to plan a wider outside margin to allow for trim.**

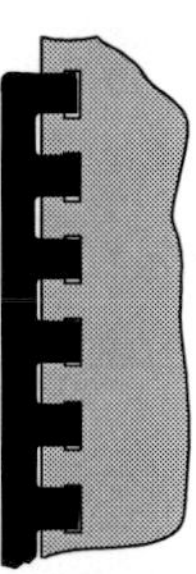

GBC binding, **spine and side view. The spine could be preprinted by silk screen.**

Spiral or plasticoil, **center and side view. Open book pages do not line up horizontally.**

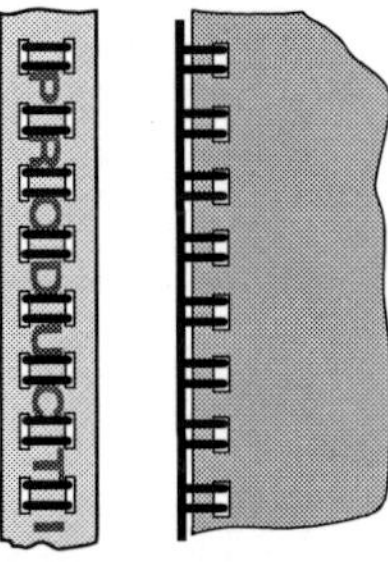

Wire-O binding, **spine and side view. Optional spine allows for simple printing.**

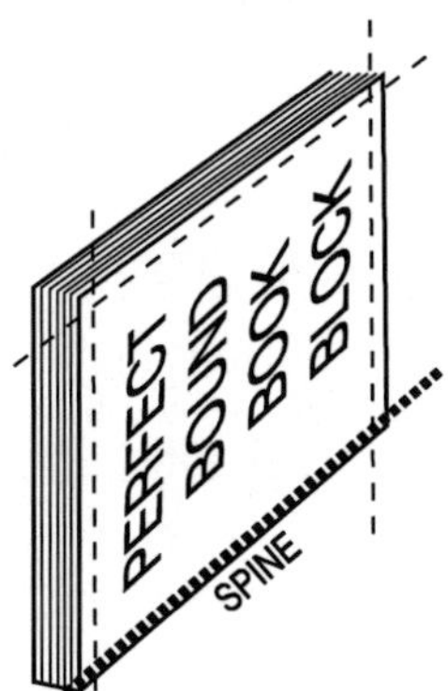

The book block would be trimmed as shown at left. The spine will be ground off during the perfect binding operation.

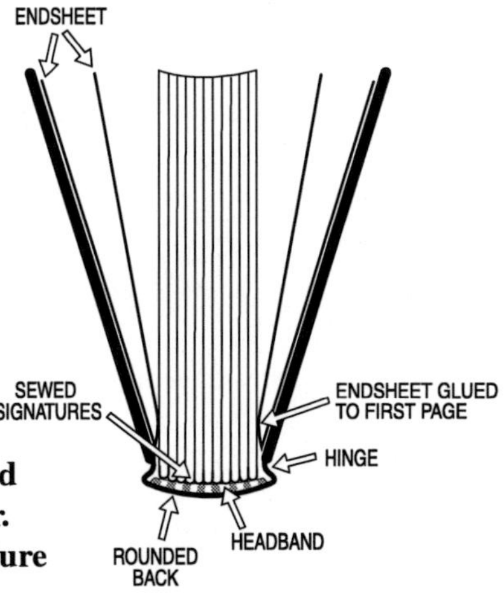

Left, **guts of a book perfect bound prior to casing in to a hard cover.** *Right,* **top view of a sewed signature case bound book.**

Diagrammatic examples of binding methods.

 TRIM GUTS ➡ 3-HOLE PUNCH ➡ BIND

- Coated paper has a clay filler among the fibers which may not absorb glue as well as uncoated paper whose substance is entirely fibrous.
- Designer/compositors should avoid having solid blocks of ink bleed to the gutter on the first and last pages of a book as glue may not adhere as well.
- Some binders cut small notches perpendicular to the spine of folded signatures to allow for greater glue penetration and thus added strength. This binding is called notch binding. It is not necessary to grind or saw off the folded spine edge of signatures with notch binding.
- Perfect bound books are trimmed three sides after binding.
- In rare instances, a customer specifies flaps on a cover that folds inside the front and back of the book. The front edge of the book cannot be trimmed after binding so the guts of the book will protrude 1/16 to 1/8 of an inch beyond the front edge of the cover. If the customer requires the pages not to protrude, the front edge must be trimmed prior to binding and the top and bottom edges trimmed in a separate operation after binding. This binding style adds expense.

GBC, SPIRAL, PLASTICOIL, WIRE-O

- GBC, spiral, plasticoil and Wire-O are sometimes called lay-flat bindings.
- These bindings are useful for manuals and instruction books that can remain open for a reader's easy reference while keeping both hands free.
- Signatures or single sheets need to be collated along with the front and back covers before binding.
- The collated book will be trimmed on all four sides before binding.
- Designer/compositor needs to allow for a trim of at least 1/8 inch off each side and set margins accordingly.
- Designer/compositor needs to allow an extra 1/4 inch on all four sides of a cover design if it is to bleed.

GBC, SPIRAL, PLASTICOIL, WIRE-O:	TRIM GUTS → 3-HOLE PUNCH → BIND

- If some workbooks or manuals need to be three-hole punched for insertion in a three-ring binder, the holes may be drilled through the collated book including cover.
- If only the text pages need to be inserted in binders, the guts may be collated and drilled before the cover is added. This extra handling can add some expense.
- Holes punched for GBC binding are rectangular to accommodate the plastic comb.
- GBC binding equipment inserts the teeth of the comb through the holes in the cover and pages.
- GBC binding is not as strong as other methods of lay-flat bindings in that the rectangular holes tear more easily and the combs can open up with hard use.
- On the other hand, a person can insert or replace pages by opening the GBC comb if those extra pages are punched.
- Spiral and plasticoil bindings are essentially the same except spiral binding uses a metal wire and plasticoil uses a plastic wire.
- A series of round holes are drilled or punched along the binding edge of books to be spiral/plasticoil bound.
- Spiral coils may be threaded through the holes in two ways:
  —preformed coils may be wound through the holes by rotating rubber rollers or by hand.
  —wire will be fed from a large spool and form the coil as it is wound through the holes.
- Coil binding is stronger than GBC because the round holes through which the coil is wound do not tear as easily.
- Metal or plastic coils have a pitch like a threaded bolt so when the book is open the pages do not line up horizontally.
- Large books (400 pages or more) require a large coil. These books should be placed in the cartons with spines alternating to avoid damaging the coils.

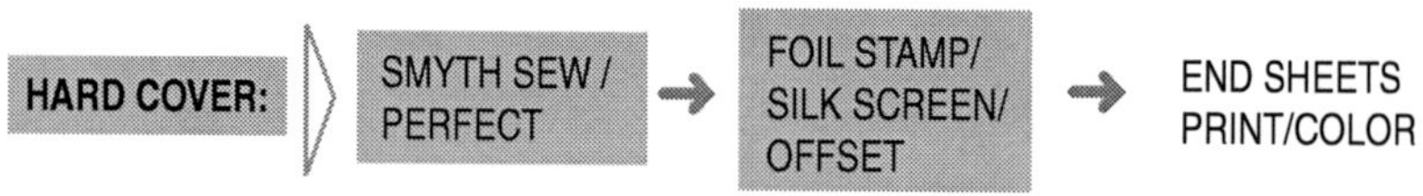

- Large coils may bend easily in shipment and require special packing and larger cartons than perfect bound or case bound books of the same thickness.
- Wire-O binding consists of a double-looped metal wire which is crimped through rectangular holes similar to GBC.
- Wire-O is stronger and not as flexible as plastic GBC.
- The cover on a Wire-O bound book can be wrapped around the spine inside of the coils, allowing a partially-visible printed spine.
- Both Wire-O and GBC bindings allow facing pages to line up horizontally as they lie flat.

HARD COVER OR CASE BINDING

- Hard cover or case binding is the method of choice for library editions, textbooks, a book subject to hard use or a book destined to be retained for posterity by the reader.
- Case binding is the most complicated method of binding and therefore the most expensive.
- Signatures prepared for case binding may be sewn or perfect bound.
- Signatures to be Smythe sewn *cannot* be perforated on the binding edge fold.
- Signatures to be perfect hard bound *can be* perforated on the binding edge before folding and collating.
- If the book is to be a split binding, *i.e.*, some Smythe sewn case bound and some perfect bound paperback, the signatures cannot be perforated on the binding edge.
- If both hard cover and paperback editions are to be perfect bound, all signatures can be perforated.
- Cover material can be cloth, plastic such as Tyvek or Kivar or paper.
- The cover may be printed by offset, silk screened or foil stamped.
- Cover material printed by offset may carry a similar design to perfect bound books. The designer/compositor needs to check what type of surface the cloth, Tyvek or paper carries.

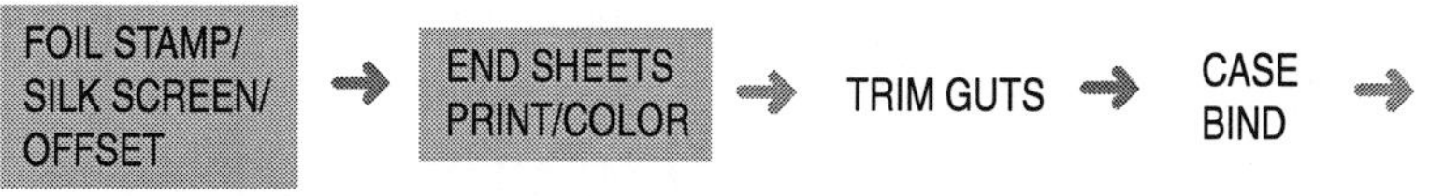

- The design for a cloth cover may not be as detailed as one printed on a smooth paper cover.
- If the cover design is printed in full on a cover to be case bound, a book jacket is usually not necessary.
- Designs can be printed by silk screen. This method does not allow for as fine detail as offset printing.
- If a case bound book is to have a jacket, the title and author's name alone are foil stamped on the cover and the spine. Sometimes this information is stamped only on the spine. The publisher's logo may also be stamped on the spine.
- Type set for stamping should be large with clean lines so the image will stamp clearly.
- Stamping foil comes in a variety of colors in addition to the traditional silver and gold.
- Stamping foil can be either metallic or pigment, with metallic displaying a brighter and cleaner image.
- The designer/compositor must allow for a larger bleed area and wider spine than for a paper perfect bound book.
- The printer should notify the binder of the thickness of the book block or send a dummy copy of the book to the binder.
- The binder should furnish a layout diagram with cover dimensions to the designer/compositor before the cover design is completed.
- For Smythe-sewn books, individual signatures are sewn with thread in the center fold of each signature.
- Sewn signatures are oversewn together with more thread on the backs to form a book block.
- The pre-binding preparation for perfect hard bound books is the same as for paper perfect books.
- Endsheets for either type of case bound book can be white or colored paper and may be printed on one side.
- The size of the endsheets after folding will be the same size as the untrimmed signatures.

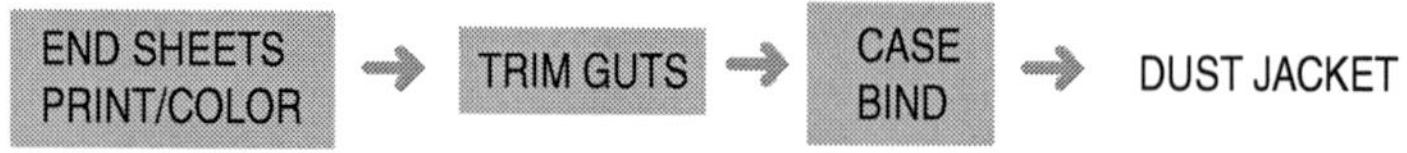

- Endsheets are folded in half and attached to the front and back signatures of a book block with a strip of glue approximately 1/4 inch wide.
- The entire book block, including endsheets, is 3-side trimmed.
- A strip of loosely woven cloth, or gauze, called a super is glued to the spine of the book block.
- The designer may choose colored cloth headbands to be attached to top and bottom of the spine of the book block before casing in.
- Covers are prepared by gluing the printed or stamped cover onto three pieces of cardboard. The front and back boards are thick—about .070 to .1 inch depending on size of book and number of pages. The spine has a thinner piece of cardboard about .010 in thickness. The front, back and spine boards are separated by a hinge area.
- The printed or stamped cover material is glued to the boards and wrapped around all four sides.
- Hard covers extend about 1/8 inch beyond the top, front and bottom edges of the signature block.
- The design has to be large enough to extend past all four edges of the boards, wrap around the edge and tuck under the endsheets.
- The spine width on a hard cover has to allow for the thickness of the book block plus the thickness of the front and back covers.
- Layout of the front cover design has to take into account the hinge area between the front board and spine.
- The book block and cover are bound together by a casing-in machine which glues the endsheets to the inside surface of the boards.
- The only thing holding the book to the cover is the 1/4 inch strip of glue fastening the endsheet to the first page and last page of the book block.
- Some book designers set a half-title page in front of the full title page for case bound books. The endsheet then glues to the

half-title page thus avoiding distortion of the title page. A blank page at the back of the book block makes for a neater look after gluing also.

- Case bound books can have a three-piece cover, *i.e.* the front and back covers would be a different material or different color than the spine. The material covering the spine crosses the hinges and overlaps the front and back cover by one inch or more.
- Case bound books may have either rounded or flat spines.

DUST JACKETS

- Design for dust jackets has to allow for the full case bound area plus about 3.5 to 4 inches for flaps to tuck inside each of the front and back covers.
- Jackets are a marketing tool as much as a protector of the cloth cover underneath.
- Attaching jackets to a book is a hand operation.
- Design, printing and attaching dust jackets adds a significant expense to book production.
- On rare occasions, perfect bound paperback books may be manufactured with front and back flaps to simulate a dust jacket.
- There are two options for handling the guts of a paperback book with flaps:
  —The book block must protrude slightly beyond the front edge so the folds on the flaps will not be trimmed off after binding.
  —The book block may be trimmed before the cover is attached. This method requires special handling and is therefore more expensive than flush-cut covers.

Ancillary Materials

By definition, ancillary means "subordinate, auxiliary or supplementary." In book publishing, ancillary material refers to instructor's guides, modules or extracts that may be sold separately from a related text or given to a customer free as part of a comprehensive package. These items might also be called collateral material.

Manufacture of CDs and DVDs does not fall in the category of printing but the inclusion of these items with a book may involve the printer and binder.

Postcards, bookmarks or other printed items may be printed at the same time as the covers to utilize wasted blank areas on a sheet.

INSTRUCTOR'S GUIDES

- Teachers utilizing textbooks and laboratory manuals in the classroom or laboratory may be furnished with teacher's guides.
- If there are exercises in the textbook or manual that require students to write answers in blank spaces, these exercises could be grouped together, appropriate answers imprinted, and bound as a booklet for the instructor.
- Any guides or supplementary material that are to be shrink wrapped together with a textbook should be the same size or smaller.
- Supplementary materials to be given away as a value-added incentive should be produced as economically as possible., *i.e.*, it might be possible to utilize saddle stitching and a self-cover.

MODULES

- Some educational materials are modular, *i.e.*, consist of a number of topics that can be collated in unique arrangements for specific customers.
- Carefully planning modules to comprise an 8-, 16-, or 32-page signature would facilitate economical collating and binding.

- If modules are to be rearranged in different order for specific customers, page numbering should start with one at the beginning of each module.
- Modules may be titled in such a way that they will be usable even if in different order, *i.e.*, not carry a number.
- A copyright notice should appear on the bottom of the first page of each module.
- Each unique collection of modules collated into book form requires a separate ISBN number.

EXTRACTS OR TEARSHEETS

- If a few pages of a book are to be used as part of a promotional package, it would be most economical to overrun the selected signatures during printing.
- The designer and author should prepare for this while the book is in composition to see if the material can fit in one signature.
- Tearsheets should be designed to start on a recto page so the text on previous pages will not be removed.

CDs, DVDs

- If a booklet is to be inserted into a jewel case with the CD, the designer/compositor might plan the design to coordinate with the cover design of the book it accompanies.
- If the CD/DVD is to be inserted inside a book, the binder may glue a sleeve inside the back cover of either a perfect bound or case bound book.
- The sleeve for the CD would normally be plain paper or plastic but could be printed if the publisher desires.
- Information and art may be printed directly on the CD or on a thin label affixed to the face of the disk. Be aware that some disk drives are very shallow and may not accommodate a CD with a paper label.

— INSTRUCTOR'S GUIDES — MODULES — EXTRACTS OR TEARSHEETS
— CDs, DVDs — POSTCARDS, BOOKMARKS

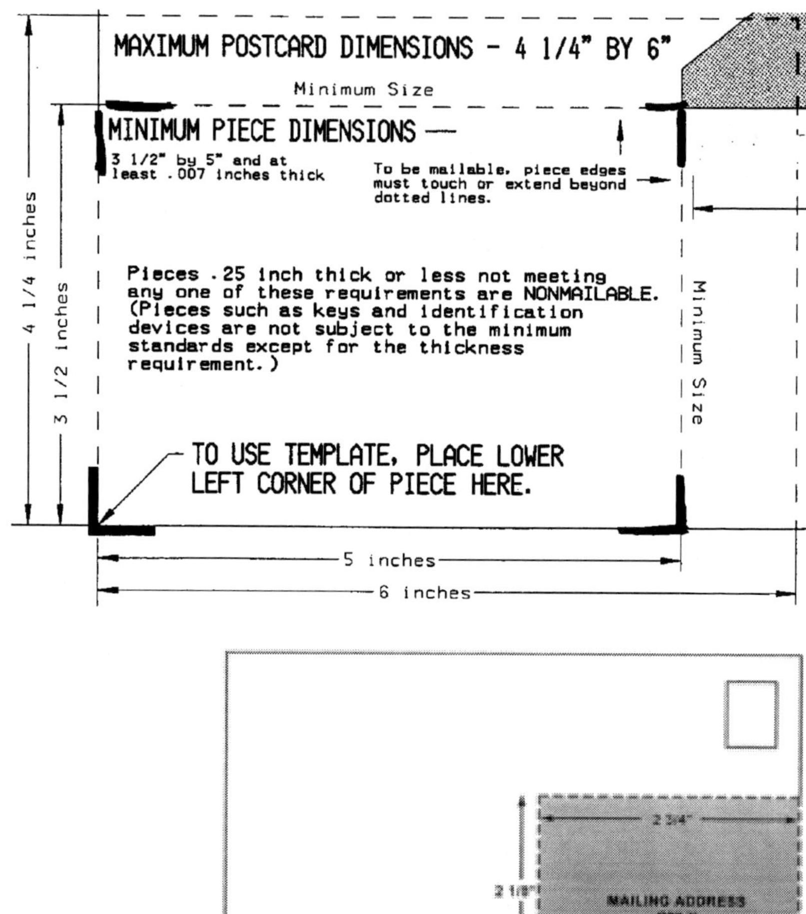

Size restrictions for postcards according to U.S. postal regulations. These examples are greatly reduced. Full-size guidelines and templates are available from any post office.

POSTCARDS, BOOKMARKS

- Promotional items such as postcards, bookmarks or other items may be printed utilizing some of the extra space on a cover sheet.
- The copy and art for these items should be planned by the author and designer/compositor while the cover design is being developed by consulting the printer.
- The designer/compositor needs to check postal regulations for minimum and maximum postcard sizes allowable.
- An overrun of the actual cover may be used as a mailer.
- An advertising message may be printed on the blank side of the cover.
- According to postal regulations for postcards, maximum dimensions for postcard mailing rate is 4.25 X 6.
- Covers up to 6 X 9 inches may be mailed as postcards at first class rate.
- Bookmarks have no dimensional restrictions.
- Consider printing information on bookmarks that will entice the customer to retain them. For example, a book on weather might contain a table with temperature conversions. A travel book might include a mileage chart.

Shipping and Order Fulfillment

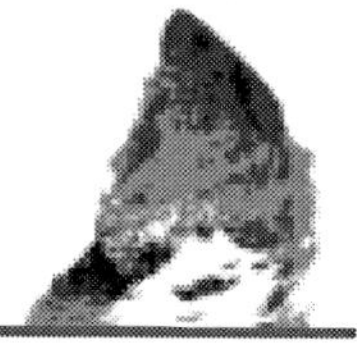

SHRINK-WRAP BATCHES	→	CARTONS (LABELS)	→	SKIDS/ SHRINK-WRAP/ DROP-SHIP	FULL OR PARTIAL SHIPMENTS F.O.B. MANUFACTURER

The publisher should consider shipping and order fulfillment from the beginning of a book project. Some decisions will affect cost while others will simply be based on convenience.

SHRINK-WRAP BATCHES

- Shrink-wrapping batches of books before placing them in cartons will be done by the bindery.
- The decision whether or not to shrink-wrap batches of books in cartons depends on how much the books will be handled.
- If whole skids will be shipped directly to the publisher's warehouse, shrink-wrapping individual books or small batches may not be necessary.
- Cover coating is a factor in the decision whether or not to shrink-wrap batches, *i.e.*, varnished covers may be prone to scratches due to abrasion in shipping, while UV coated or laminated books may be abrasion resistant.
- If the printer/binder will store the finished books in cartons on skids, shrink-wrapping of batches may not be necessary.

CARTONS AND LABELS

- Short press runs for POD books will require very few cartons. Labeling might be a simple handwritten notation on the boxes.
- If cartons are to be stored by either the printer or fulfillment warehouse along with other titles, careful labeling is required.
- Labels should indicate ISBN, author name(s), abbreviated title, quantity of books in a carton and publisher's name.
- If books will be stored high on racks in a warehouse, labels with large type will be easier to read from floor level.

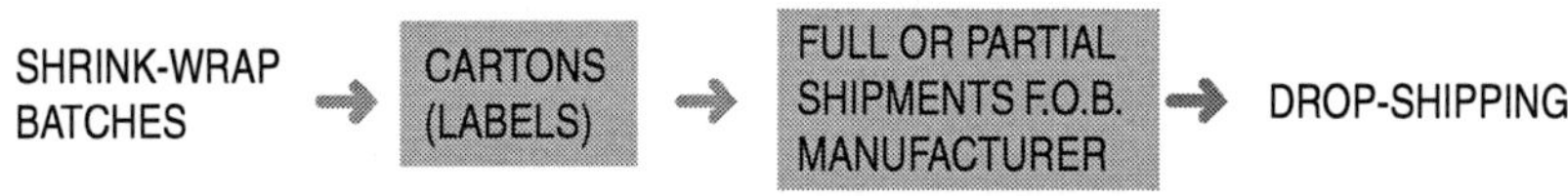

0-9679349-3-1
LUNDIN
Book Prod. Encap.
60 **books**
Mori Studio Southwest

Book Production
Encapsulated

Mori Studio

60 copies

These images are approximately 25% of actual label size.

The label on the left would be easier to read from the ground floor if cartons are stacked high on shelves.

- The publisher may consider furnishing printed carton labels printed with the most useful information for their company.
- Check with the printer/binder to get an estimate of how many books will fit in a carton.
- The publisher can run off labels on a laser or inkjet printer and furnish them to the printer/binder. Check whether the supplier packing the books has a glue machine for plain labels or requires self-adhesive stock.

FULL OR PARTIAL SHIPMENTS

- The publisher should monitor deadlines carefully for material that is time-sensitive.
- If it is necessary to make several small shipments to satisfy customers instead of one large shipment, efficiency is lost and shipping cost increases.
- If it is necessary to make express shipments rather than regular freight, costs increase.
- Ascertain that the printer/binder is utilizing the most cost-effective method of shipping.

SHRINK-WRAP BATCHES → CARTONS (LABELS) → FULL OR PARTIAL SHIPMENTS F.O.B. MANUFACTURER → DROP-SHIPPING

- If the publisher has an account with a specific carrier, request that the books be transported by that carrier.
- Printers or binders with a high volume of shipping may receive a discounted rate from transport companies.
- Printers or binders often pass along shipping charges to a publisher at cost, *i.e.*, with no markup.

DROP SHIPPING

- Choice of a book manufacturer may be predicated on geographic location.
- Order fulfillment from a central location may save shipping costs for books with nationwide distribution.

Wrap-up Activities

At this stage, book production activities come full circle. Several of the items described in the wrap-up section need to be initiated early in the production cycle and the remainder completed upon the book's publication.

BOWKER (ISBN)

- The International Standard Book Number system is a voluntary system for publishers administered by R.R. Bowker.
- Although voluntary, any publisher not assigning an ISBN to a book is instantly labeled as unprofessional.
- The ISBN system is utilized by all bookstores, distributors, wholesalers and libraries to order and catalog books.
- Sales outlets would not be likely to order books that do not have an ISBN.
- Ordering ISBN from R.R. Bowker should be one of the first steps taken by a new publisher even before a manuscript is finished.
- Publishers can order a series of numbers from Bowker which are to be used only by the publisher to which assigned.
- The minimum number of ISBN that may be purchased is ten.
- This is the address of the U.S. ISBN Agency:

  > U.S. ISBN Agency
  > 630 Central Avenue
  > New Providence, NJ 07974
  > Tel: 877-310-7333
  > Fax: 908-219-0188
  > e-mail: isbn-san@bowker.com

- To get complete information about the ISBN and the registration process, check www.isbn.org/ on the internet.

| BOWKER (ISBN) | COPYRIGHT APPLICATION | LIBRARY OF CONGRESS |

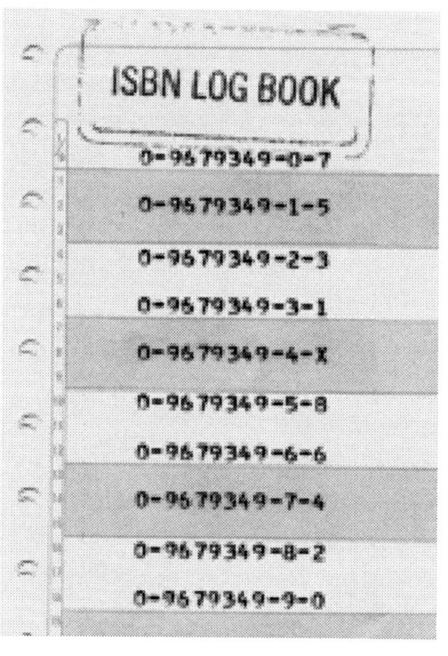

This is an example of a batch of ten ISBNs furnished by R.R. Bowker. ISBNs may be ordered in blocks of 10, 100, 1000 or 10,000. The regular processing fee at the time of this writing for a block of 10 is $225 plus a $14.95 publisher registration fee.

- There are two ways to register a title with R.R.Bowker:
  —send an Advance Book Information form well ahead of the publication date and preferably as soon as you have assigned a number to a publication
  —Fill out a Title Registration form online after publication.
- The publisher and designer/compositor need to work together to be sure that the proper ISBN appears on a book.
- R.R. Bowker recommends that the ISBN should appear on the copyright page of the book, on the back cover and spine of a perfect bound paperback and on the back cover of a casebound book. If the case bound book has a jacket, the ISBN would be printed on the jacket.
- In practice, designers and publishers rarely print the ISBN on the spine of a book.
- After publication and registration, a book title meeting R.R. Bowker's criteria will be listed in *Books in Print.*

BOWKER (ISBN)   COPYRIGHT   LIBRARY OF
                   APPLICATION   CONGRESS

COPYRIGHT

- According to copyright law, an unpublished manuscript is protected as the creator's work even without registration.
- If the author/publisher wishes to register copyright for a book in the manuscript stage, one copy of the manuscript must be sent to the copyright office along with a completed Form TX or Short Form TX and a payment of the current fee.
- Normally, copyright would be registered after publication and two copies sent to the copyright office along with Form TX or Short Form TX and the registration fee.
- The address of the copyright office is:

      Library of Congress
      Copyright Office
      101 Independence Avenue, S.E.
      Washington, DC 20559-6000

- The copyright notice can be placed on the literary work as soon as it is created, but a certificate of registration may not be returned to the author/publisher from the copyright office until four or five months after submission.
- The copyright notice must appear on the title page or the reverse thereof. The symbol © must be used by all members of the International Copyright Convention.
- Publishers uusally add "All rights reserved" after the copyright notice and a paragraph spelling out possible infringements.
- It is suggested that the author/publisher be quite certain of a publication date before registering a copyright. If production on a book is delayed and the final product does not come out until the following year, the work may be considered outdated by sales outlets or end users.
- If a book is published within the last few months of a year, publishers frequently indicate the following year on the copyright notice.
- Under current copyright law, the work is protected for the life of the author plus fifty years.

BOWKER (ISBN)   COPYRIGHT APPLICATION   LIBRARY OF CONGRESS

LIBRARY OF CONGRESS CONTROL NUMBER

- The Library of Congress has a criteria for the types of books that can carry a LCCN.
- In general, a book may be eligible for a LCCN if it is a title "likely to be acquired by U.S. libraries" or "most likely to be selected and cataloged by the Library of Congress for its own collections."
- The publisher can get much information about eligibility for participation in either the CIP or PCN programs on the internet at: lcweb.loc.gov/
- If a Library of Congress Control Number is to be assigned to a book, the information should be acquired early in the book production cycle so the number can be typeset on the copyright page of the book before printing.
- The Library of Congress' description of the book exactly as shown on library cards may be printed on the copyright page of a book. The description must be printed line for line with the same indents as copy provided by the Library of Congress.


```
          Library of Congress Cataloging-in-Publication Data

Tigner, Richard W.
     Into the wild blue : remembrances of World War II / Richard W.
  Tigner.
        p.   cm.
    ISBN 0-8087-7813-7
     1. Tigner, Richard W.  2. World War, 1939-1945--Aerial operations,
  American.  3. World War, 1939-1945--Personal narratives, American.
  4. United States.  Army Air Forces--Biography.  5. United States.
  Army Air Forces--Aerial gunners--Biography.   I. Title.
  D790.T55  1992
  940.54'4973--dc20                                           92-39540
                                                                  CIP
```


This is an example of a Library of Congress Cataloguing-in-Publication notice that would be printed on the copyright page of a book. The format must be followed line for line when typesetting.

BOWKER (ISBN)   COPYRIGHT APPLICATION   LIBRARY OF CONGRESS

- If a PCN is obtained, this line only is printed on the copyright page:

    Library of Congress Control Number: 0000000000

- One complimentary copy of the completed book should be sent to:

    Library of Congress
    Cataloging in Publication Division
    101 Independence Avenue S.E.
    Washington, DC 20540-4320

- No form or fee is required to be sent with the published book. The CIP or PCN application form would already be on file at the Library of Congress.

Planning Future Production

RERUNS

- Check with the printer to arrange for storage of films and/or plates if the book has been printed by conventional offset.
- When getting a printing and binding estimate, ask for an estimate for reruns also. Note that most book manufacturers' estimates will only be guaranteed for 30 to 60 days. However, a rerun estimate will give the publisher an idea of the relative cost savings of a straight rerun over the first printing which includes all pre-press and make-ready charges.
- On digitally-printed books, the publisher should check to see how long the printer will retain RIP files.
- The publisher and/or the designer/compositor should always save at least one copy of the final version of a book in the page layout mode along with a copy of the PDF conversion.
- Remember that PDF files cannot be altered, so any corrections must be made in the page layout application and a new PDF file created.
- If a correction does not cause copy to reflow from one page to another, the printer may be able to make a new PDF file of the corrected page only and furnish it to the printer for replacement in the RIPed file.
- Always identify stored files clearly. Depending on how many letters the page layout program allows, the filename could show understandable abbreviations of the title, author name and date or year of publication. Whoever is storing the files could also use an abbreviated ISBN as part of the identification. For example if the publisher's ISBN is "0-9679349-3-1," the identification could be abbreviated to "3-1" since the first eight digits will always be the same for that particular publisher.

REVISIONS: STORE PAGE FILES, PDF FILES

- Remember that a straight rerun or rerun with minimal corrections will retain the initial copyright date.
- A rerun with minimal or no changes retains the original ISBN and copyright notice.

REVISIONS

- The same procedures for RIP and PDF file storage and file identification apply for books that will be revised.
- For offset-printed books, it is not necessary to store negs and plates if a book is certain to contain extensive revisions in the second edition.
- If there are minimum revisions planned, some film might be salvaged if the revisions do not cause a reflow of the page layout.
- Again, the electronic page layout files should be stored by the publisher and/or the designer/compositor.
- Some publishers arrange for a second set of the files to be stored in a separate location to minimize loss from fire, flood or natural disaster.
- As a rule of thumb, if 20% to 30% or more of a book's text is changed, a new copyright date can be assigned.
- The original copyright date and all subsequent revised dates are displayed in sequence on the copyright page, usually beginning with the most recent.
- If a book is revised and carries a new copyright date, a new ISBN must be assigned.

Print on Demand
and eBooks

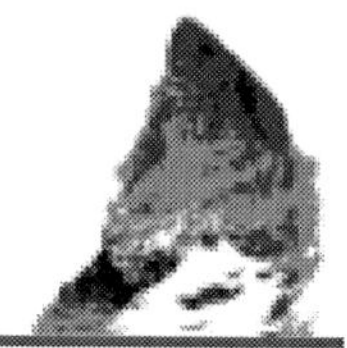

Most of the manuscript preparation, copyediting, proofreading, design and composition activities discussed in earlier chapters of this booklet would still apply to books prepared for print on demand. The print on demand (POD) concept touts the ability to print books as needed after an order is received. Digital printing technology has definitely made it feasible to produce a small number of books at a cost that allows a competitive retail price. Theoretically, even orders for one book can be fulfilled. In practice, few POD printers can produce just one or two copies of a book at a competitive price in a first printing. Print-on-demand may also be called "just-in-time" printing.

Independent publishers and authors desiring to control the design/composition process can do so through all the steps prior to submitting electronic files to a POD printer. Author/publishers less comfortable with preparing their own material prepress, can buy POD packages with a wide choice of publishing services.

MANUSCRIPT PREP AND
AUTHOR-CONTROLLED PREPRESS

- Author/publishers intending to sell their books through conventional retail channels and with their own imprint need to obtain a series of ISBN from R.R. Bowker.
- Many POD services offer to furnish an ISBN to clients who contract printing.
- Author/publishers with only one or two titles may find it more economical to let the POD service provide an ISBN rather than spending about $240 for a set of ten unique numbers.
- If the POD service furnishes an ISBN, that printer's imprint will appear on the title page as publisher.
- Author/publishers intending to sell books to libraries, and whose works may have wide commercial acceptance, should apply for a Preassigned Control Number (PCN) from the Library of Congress.

"Got a book in you?'
"Is there an author in you?"
"Most everyone has a book in them."

These are some of the catch lines proffered by print-on-demand services.

- The author/publisher must obtain permissions if text or illustrative copy is borrowed from someone else's published material.
- If the POD service is contracted only for printing and binding, the printer usually prefers PDF files with all art and photos in place.
- Short-run printing technology allows covers to be printed in full color.
- Cover art should be saved as CMYK before converting to PDF.
- Pages should be composed in a standard layout program such as QuarkXPress, PageMaker, Adobe InDesign or Ventura Publisher.
- Some printers will not accept final page layout in Microsoft Word PDF files or will charge extra to handle those files.
- Photos to be printed black only should be converted to grayscale before placing them in the layout.
- Author/publishers requiring only printing and binding services should have their material copyedited and proofread carefully by someone other that the author before going to press.
- Author/publishers contracting only for printing and binding will be responsible for their own advertising, marketing and fulfillment of orders.
- Author/publishers should obtain estimates from three to five POD services.
- Different POD services can require from 10 working days up to four or five weeks to complete the first printing.
- Straight reprints can be produced in three to five days by some services.

FULL SERVICE PRINT ON DEMAND

- Full service POD may work well for an author/publisher who is not familiar with book production or simply does not want to bother with production details between submitting a manuscript and holding a bound book.

- The author/publisher should explore services offered by at least five POD full-service suppliers.
- A large number of POD services can be found on the internet by simply searching for "print on demand."
- The lowest bidder may not always be the best choice for a particular author/publisher.
- A study of POD full service vendors indicates the following:
  - The POD service usually requires a final manuscript in Microsoft Word along with a hard copy.
  - Some suppliers will accept electronic files by e-mail.
  - Up-front fees range from $150 to $3500 depending on services included.
  - Sometimes the ISBN is included, sometimes not.
  - Copyediting is not part of the package without an additional fee.
  - Specifications for most POD packages are for 5.5 X 8.5 or 6 X 9 inch trim size, 50# or 60# white paper stock and an estimated 100 to 250 pages.
  - Most POD packages include page layout in one of two or three standard no-frills formats.
  - The author/publisher can choose from several standard cover design formats or pay extra for custom designs.
  - Covers are printed on 10 point coated one side (C1S) stock in full color.
  - Some printers furnish only 10 to 20 copies of the book as part of the initial contract.
  - Printers charging higher fees include an initial printing of 50 to 500 books.
  - More copies will be printed for purchase by the author/publisher as needed.
  - The production package often includes a run of up to 500 sell-sheet flyers, postcards and bookmarks.
  - Several POD service companies will attempt to place copies with Barnes and Noble, Amazon or Borders bookstores.
  - Some services include listing of titles on their web pages.
- Subsidy publishers are POD services which print a set number of books for the basic fee and pay a "royalty" to the author as

books are sold through their channels. Actually, the royalties are usually incremental rebates off the author/publisher's own initial investment.

- Some subsidy publishers will reprint books at their own expense if a title sells a minimum of 500 to 1000 copies in a year.
- Royalties are advertised as a percentage of net income or of retail price.
- Author/publishers should carefully analyze royalties advertised as a high percentage of net income. Net income is what is left after bookstore discounts and manufacturing costs are deducted from the sales price.

Example:	Retail price:	$10.00
	50% bookstore discount:	(5.00)
	Manufacturing cost:	(3.00)
	Net income:	2.00
	75% of net income:	1.50/book
	40% of net income:	.80/book

eBOOKS

eBooks are books designed to be downloaded to a client's computer or handheld device and viewed on a screen. While some titles are written exclusively for the electronic format, many of the documents are electronic versions of books already in print. Traditional print publishers are increasingly converting titles to eBooks as an extension of their marketing efforts.

An author/publisher with an existing website, or the computer knowledge to construct one, can post preformatted books on their own site. A number of service bureaus exist who accept manuscripts, convert the files to eBook format for their own websites, and pay royalties to authors as books are sold.

MANUSCRIPT PREP FOR eBOOKS

- The author/publisher or the service bureau needs to obtain an ISBN from R.R. Bowker as with printed books.
- If the book already exists in print, a new ISBN must be assigned to the electronic version.
- A copyright notice should appear prominently on or after the title page.

- An eBook manuscript must just as carefully edited and proof-read as a print edition.
- Even though an eBook is intended to be read on a screen, it is formatted much like a conventional book with title page, copyright notice, preface, table of contents, chapter headings and subheadings.
- A professional-looking cover design is essential to attract readers of eBooks as well as print books.
- Most eBook publishers insist that manuscripts be submitted in Microsoft Word or Rich Text Format (RTF).
- Pages should not be numbered in the Word/RTF document submitted for eBook formatting.
- There should be no running headers on manuscript copy.
- Italics should be used for emphasis, as necessary, but words should not be underlined.
- Most services accepting manuscripts insist that Word/RTF text be set in 10 or 12 point Times Roman with chapter headings and subheads set in 14 point lowercase with initial caps.
- The Word/RTF document should have consistent paragraph indents by tab, not spacebar.
- If the Word/RTF document is to be reformatted by the website service, check whether art or photos should be submitted as separate jpg, tif or eps files rather than embedded in text.
- Most eBook publishers prefer receiving manuscripts via e-mail attachment.
- Some eBook publishers suggest that documents be as small as 75 KB while others will accept documents of not more than 3 MB.
- Cover designs may have the same visual elements as for a printed book with the following exceptions:
    — No spine is necessary.
    — The front and back covers are separate pages.
    — No barcode is needed.

FINAL FORMAT FOR eBOOK READERS

- The predominant eBook formats are PDF, HTML and RTF and readable on the widest range of hardware.
- The page layout for most eBooks is very similar to printed books except there are no verso pages.

- Handheld readers usually have screens with a larger vertical dimension than horizontal to simulate conventional book page proportions.
- The eBook designer may adapt the page to the proportions of a computer screen, *i.e.,* wider than tall.
- eBook pages should have equal margins left and right since pages will be viewed one at a time and not as facing spreads.
- An author/publisher with complete page layouts in InDesign, QuarkXPress, PageMaker, etc., with all headings and art in place, may save their documents in PDF or HTML formats for direct placement on the internet.
- Final PDF or HTML documents should be limited to 2 or 3 MB.

    Two examples of existing eBook document sizes:
    — *The DaVinci Code,* by Dan Brown, 454 pages in hard cover; text only, not illustrated;
    downloads 1175 KB as an eBook, Adobe Reader format.
    — *The Wonderful Wizard of Oz,* by L. Frank Baum, 217 pages with some full page illustrations in print;
    downloads 2.8 MB as an eBook, Adobe Reader format.

- Reader software, such as Adobe Reader, which allows computers or handheld devices to read PDF files, is often furnished free to eBook customers.
- eBook reader hardware costs can range from about $70 to $300 or more.
- Most Palm Pilots can be utilized as eBook readers.
- eBook readers have rechargeable batteries or adapters for in-home electrical outlets or auto cigarette lighters.
- An author/publisher with eBook marketing success can reap a greater profit than from a printed edition for several reasons:
    — There is no printing or binding cost.
    — No physical inventory is necessary.
    — Page layout and design costs can be minimal if simple standard designs are acceptable.

Two of many resources on the internet that explain eBook preparation in greater detail:
www.publishyourownebooks.com/write-an-ebook
www.adobe.com/epaper/tips/acr5ebook/pdfs/eBook.pdf

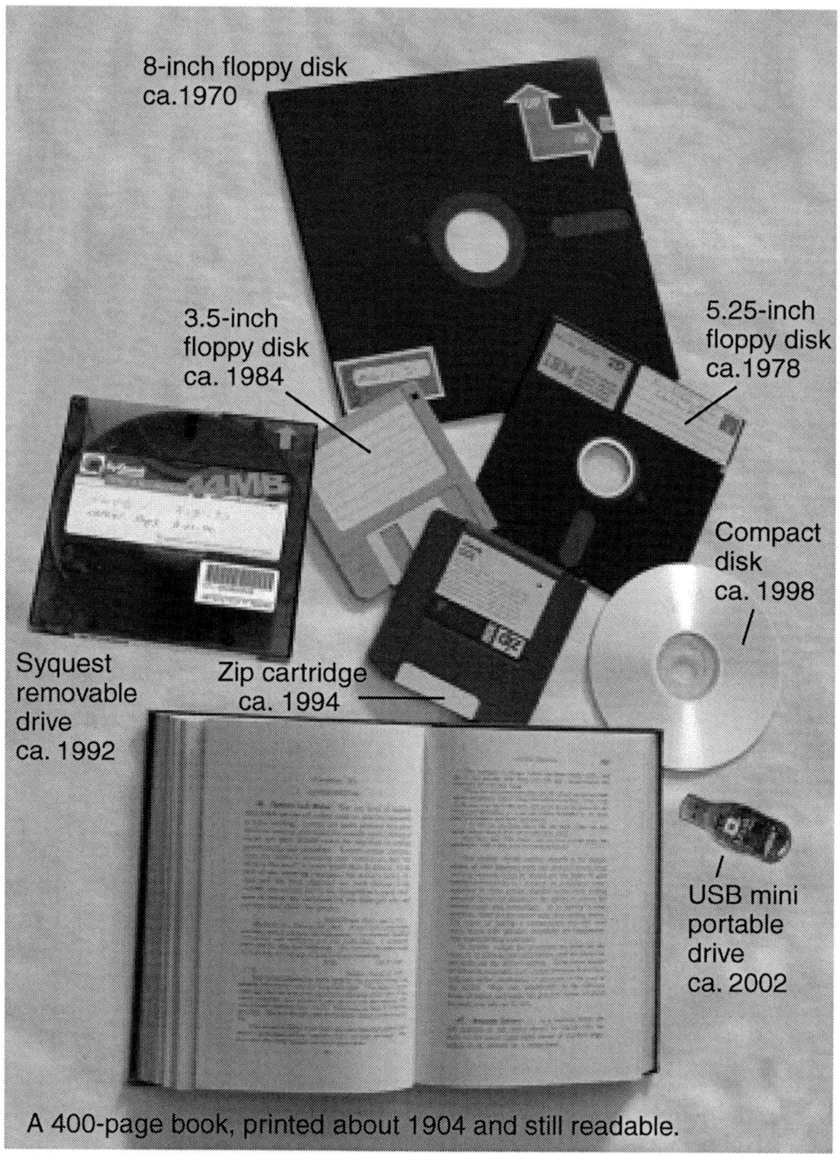

A 400-page book, printed about 1904 and still readable.

Storage of data for posterity—but is it retrievable? The capacity for storing data electronically has increased a thousand fold in less than 20 years. Hardware changes and becomes outdated. Disks are no longer readable in new equipment. The printed book will survive all the changes in electronic technology and its data will be retrievable for decades, still communicating with generations to come.